To:
From:
Date:

DAILY PRAYERS
FOR MORNING AND EVENING
Inspiration & Encouragement for Teen Girls
BARBOUR
PUBLISHING

Print ISBN 979-8-89151-132-3

Devotional thoughts and prayers are inspired by *365 Encouraging Prayers for Morning and Evening* published by Barbour Publishing, Inc.

Published by Barbour Publishing, Inc., 1810 Barbour Drive, Uhrichsville, Ohio 44683, www.barbourbooks.com

Our mission is to inspire the world with the life-changing message of the Bible.

Printed in China.

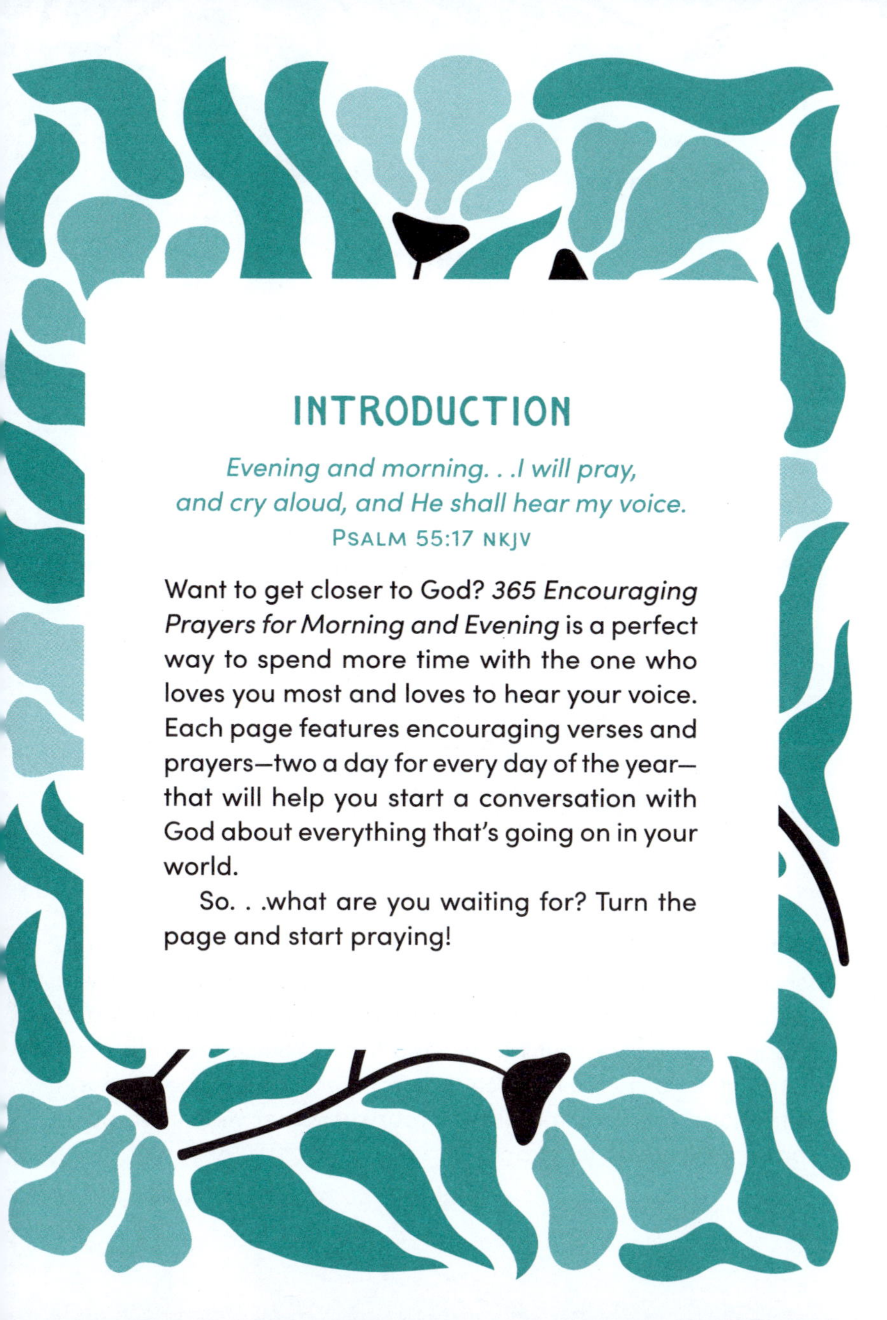

INTRODUCTION

Evening and morning. . .I will pray,
and cry aloud, and He shall hear my voice.
Psalm 55:17 NKJV

Want to get closer to God? *365 Encouraging Prayers for Morning and Evening* is a perfect way to spend more time with the one who loves you most and loves to hear your voice. Each page features encouraging verses and prayers—two a day for every day of the year—that will help you start a conversation with God about everything that's going on in your world.

So. . .what are you waiting for? Turn the page and start praying!

MORNING

NO ONE LIKE HIM

Who is like the LORD our God, who dwells on high?

PSALM 113:5 NKJV

Heavenly Father, today I'm grateful for all You are. Your character never changes—*never*! You are perfect holiness and love. Your truthfulness is indisputable, and Your power is proven. Because of who You are, I believe and trust in You. I worship You today not just for the awesome works You've done but for the pure awesomeness of Your nature.

EVENING

GRACE FOR EVERYTHING

But he gives us more grace.

JAMES 4:6 NIV

Father, I'm thankful for Your grace—the undeserved favor You show me through Jesus. Without Your grace, I wouldn't even be able to approach You. Thank You for forgiving my sins and adopting me into Your family. And thank You so much for that extra dose of perseverance that You keep giving me in tough situations. I'm so grateful that Your resources never run out. I praise You today for grace.

MORNING

COME CLOSER, BELOVED

In him and through faith in him we may approach God with freedom and confidence.

EPHESIANS 3:12 NIV

Lord, You are the God of the universe, yet You ask me to come closer. You say I can approach You with freedom and confidence. I praise You for Your Son, Jesus, who allows me this access to You. I am small, but I want to know You better. I am weak, but You have power to spare. Help me come closer and closer.

EVENING

A POSITIVE ATTITUDE

"For the LORD searches all hearts and understands all the intent of the thoughts."

1 CHRONICLES 28:9 NKJV

Lord, You see how I really think and feel. Help me let go of the things that have hurt me. I don't want those things to be my focus. Let me focus instead on You and Your plans for my life. Help me do everything without grumbling, complaining, or pointing fingers at others. Fill me with Your joy, and strengthen me with Your love.

DAY 3

MORNING

HEARD FROM HEAVEN

"If my people. . .will humble themselves and pray and seek my face and turn from their wicked ways, then I will hear from heaven."

2 CHRONICLES 7:14 NIV

Father, I thank You that You are always listening for my voice. You know it out of billions of others. My words are not just spoken to the empty air, but You give them Your attention. Please forgive my sins, Lord, and help me to live for You. Thank You for hearing and forgiving.

EVENING

GUARDING MY MIND

You will keep in perfect peace those whose minds are steadfast, because they trust in you.

ISAIAH 26:3 NIV

As I spend time with You, Lord, I learn to trust You. Your Word is my weapon to fight negative thoughts. I will be careful about the things I see and hear because I know they can affect my thinking. Help me guard my mind. Help me focus on the truth so that no negative thought will have power over me.

MORNING

EVERYTHING IS POSSIBLE

"Abba, Father, all things are possible for You."
MARK 14:36 NKJV

How amazing! You, my Father, are the Creator of the universe! Your infinite creativity formed everything, everywhere. I know I can trust in Your might and Your abilities; there's nothing in heaven or on earth that You can't handle. Forgive me when I try to take things into my own hands. Since You made the world, I know You can take care of my small life!

EVENING

A TEACHABLE ATTITUDE

Listen to my words. Turn your ear to my sayings.
. . . Keep them in the center of your heart.
For they are life to those who find them.
PROVERBS 4:20–22 NLV

Holy Spirit, be my teacher. Guide me as I read the Bible. Show me how to let go of any selfishness or stubbornness and listen to Your direction. I'll go where You want me to go today. Help me focus my heart and energy on Your instruction.

DAY 5

MORNING

RECEIVING JESUS

Yet to all who did receive him, to those who believed in his name, he gave the right to become children of God.

John 1:12 NIV

Lord, I believe in Your name. Help me believe even more. Take away the doubts that the world shouts at me every day. Keep my eyes focused on You, even when troubles come. Keep my ears tuned to Your voice, especially when I'm tempted to listen to other voices. I welcome You into my heart.

EVENING

SHOWING MERCY

Never pay back someone for the bad he has done to you. Let the anger of God take care of the other person.

Romans 12:19 NLV

Lord, when others treat me unfairly, judge me, or take something I feel I deserved, I want to get even. I want to fight for what is mine, but then I feel You urging me to choose a different response. Showing mercy is difficult sometimes, but with Your love and grace, I can.

MORNING

AMAZING FORGIVENESS

In Him we have redemption through His blood, the forgiveness of sins, according to the riches of His grace.
EPHESIANS 1:7 NKJV

Lord, thank You for forgiveness. Many people struggle with guilt because of what they've done in the past, but I know my past is redeemed because of Christ's sacrifice for me. Your forgiveness is so amazing! Even though I don't deserve it, You pour it out freely and lovingly. Because You have chosen to pardon me, I bless Your name today.

EVENING

STRENGTH IN GOD

The LORD is my strength and shield. I trust him with all my heart. He helps me, and my heart is filled with joy.
PSALM 28:7 NLT

Lord, You are my strength and my shield. You give me courage to meet challenges. You build me up, leading me to places I never would have dreamed possible. You are the friend who never leaves me, the guide who walks ahead of me. With You in my life, I can do anything.

DAY 7

MORNING

NO WORRIES

"I am leaving you with a gift—peace of mind and heart. And the peace I give is a gift the world cannot give. So don't be troubled or afraid."

JOHN 14:27 NLT

Lord, it's hard to find peace in this world. It's so noisy! But when I pray to You, especially in the quietness of the morning, my thoughts, heart, and spirit are at rest. When I sit with You, I have no worries, no troubles, no fears. You are peace.

EVENING

THE LORD ALMIGHTY

"I will be a Father to you. You will be My sons and daughters, says the All-powerful God."

2 CORINTHIANS 6:18 NLV

You, Lord God, can do all things, for You are almighty and ever present. Because You are my Father, I know I can trust You to handle every part of my life. I trust You with my past, my present, and my future. You are God, and I'm not—and I'm thankful that's the way it is.

MORNING

GO TO GOD

This is the word that came to Jeremiah from the LORD: "Go down to the potter's house, and there I will give you my message."

JEREMIAH 18:1–2 NIV

So many times, Lord, I feel like dropping to my knees and praying, but don't. Thank You that You keep calling my name again and again. Please help me trust You enough to stop what I'm doing when I hear Your call. I'm on my knees now, Lord. I'm listening to Your voice.

EVENING

GOD'S WORD IS TRUTH

Jesus said, "If you hold to my teaching, you are really my disciples. Then you will know the truth, and the truth will set you free."

JOHN 8:31–32 NIV

Lord, Your Word is true. I want to know the truth and live it. Help me look to Your solid Word, not to this world, for my life instruction manual. Thank You that You will never lead me off course, that You never lie to me, and that You always keep Your promises.

DAY 9

MORNING

A FATHER'S MERCY

I will be his father, and he shall be my son: and I will not take my mercy away from him.

1 CHRONICLES 17:13 KJV

Thank You, Lord, for never taking Your mercy away from me. No matter how many times I let You down, I can always count on You to pick me up. I don't understand this gift, but I'm thankful for it. Please show me ways to extend mercy to the people in my life.

EVENING

LIGHT FOR UNDERSTANDING

Your word is a lamp for my feet, a light on my path.

PSALM 119:105 NIV

Lord, Your Word is like a beam of light on my path through life, helping me see the way. Your words give me insight and hope, even when I can't see where I'm going or how things will turn out. I'm so glad You know the right direction. You go ahead of me, so I don't need to be afraid. I choose to follow You.

MORNING

GOD OF ALL COMFORT

Blessed be God. . .the Father of mercies, and the God of all comfort.

2 CORINTHIANS 1:3 KJV

You comfort me, Father, when my heart aches. When everything in my life seems to be going wrong and when everything in the world seems to be going wrong too, Your comfort never fails. Thank You for offering me that constant care in my life. Help me share Your comfort with others—ultimately leading them to You.

EVENING

GOD'S WORD IS POWERFUL

The word of God is alive and powerful. It is sharper than the sharpest two-edged sword, cutting between soul and spirit, between joint and marrow. It exposes our innermost thoughts and desires.

HEBREWS 4:12 NLT

I can't hide from You, Lord. *You know everything*. Although You love me as I am, the Bible—Your Word that's living and active and so powerful—helps me see what's wrong in my life. Thank You for Your grace that enables me to repent and change.

MORNING

I WILL HEAR

"Before they call I will answer;
while they are still speaking I will hear."
ISAIAH 65:24 NIV

Dear Lord, I praise You for being the God who hears. I praise You that You know my heart better than *I* do. I can relax because You are answering my prayers before I even finish praying. Help me be more like You by listening with love to the people around me. I need Your ears and Your heart, Lord. Amen.

EVENING

GOD-BREATHED WORDS

All Scripture is God-breathed and is useful for teaching, rebuking, correcting and training in righteousness, so that the servant of God may be thoroughly equipped for every good work.
2 TIMOTHY 3:16–17 NIV

Lord, Your Word tells me that You breathed life into the words that men put on parchment—the words of the Bible I read today. Teach me, Lord. Correct and train me in righteousness so that I will be ready for whatever I might face.

MORNING

A GODLY CONFIDENCE

Now this is the confidence that we have in Him, that if we ask anything according to His will, He hears us.
1 JOHN 5:14 NKJV

Dear Lord, sometimes it feels like my prayers are just a long list of wishes and You're some sort of genie. I'm so thankful that's not true. You don't give me what I want just because I want it. You give me only what lines up with Your will. Help me see what that is.

EVENING

WISDOM TO EXPLAIN

Work hard so you can present yourself to God and receive his approval. Be a good worker, one who does not need to be ashamed and who correctly explains the word of truth.
2 TIMOTHY 2:15 NLT

Lord, I want to please You. Teach me how to live so that I receive Your approval. Give me a hunger for reading the Bible so I'll know it better, and help me share what I learn. I want to be a person who correctly explains the Word of Truth.

MORNING

GOD'S GREAT LOVE

See how very much our Father loves us, for he calls us his children, and that is what we are!

1 JOHN 3:1 NLT

A good father protects his children. He loves his children unconditionally. He understands and forgives his children. He provides for his family. Lord, You are so much more than a good father—You are the *perfect* Father. Remind me that *this* is the way You love me. Thank You for loving me completely and perfectly.

EVENING

TO KNOW GOD'S WILL

We continually ask God to fill you with the knowledge of his will through all the wisdom and understanding that the Spirit gives.

COLOSSIANS 1:9 NIV

Lord, I want to know Your will for my life. Please give me understanding. Show me when to stay and when to go, when to speak and when to close my mouth. Help me see Your best for me—right now and in the future. And help me accept Your answers obediently and joyfully.

MORNING

LIGHTS

Live clean, innocent lives as children of God, shining like bright lights in a world full of crooked and perverse people.
PHILIPPIANS 2:15 NLT

Lord, I'm glad I can call You my Father. Because You live in my heart, I'm Your representative in the world. Thank You for using me for Your purpose, and thank You for filling in the gaps—I can't live as Your child without Your help! Make me a light to those around me, not so I shine but so Your awesomeness does.

EVENING

REVIVE ME!

The law of the LORD is perfect, refreshing the soul. The statutes of the LORD are trustworthy, making wise the simple.
PSALM 19:7 NIV

Lord, sometimes life gets crazy. I get so tired and stressed out from school and sports and chores. I can't wait to sit in Your presence and be refreshed. Revive my soul with Your Word. Dunk me in Your truth. Turn the dark places in my life to light so I can radiate Jesus everywhere I go.

DAY 15

MORNING

GOOD GIFTS

"So if you sinful people know how to give good gifts to your children, how much more will your heavenly Father give good gifts to those who ask him."

MATTHEW 7:11 NLT

Lord, I'm just a teenager, but I know what's a good gift and what's not. You are a loving and generous Father, and You know how to give good things better than anyone else. You give us so much! Lord, thank You for giving only good things when we ask.

EVENING

GIVE ME JOY

The Laws of the Lord are right, giving joy to the heart. The Word of the Lord is pure, giving light to the eyes.

PSALM 19:8 NLV

Lord, Your words make my heart joyful, and joy is something everybody needs. I might be happy or I might not be happy, but Your joy sticks around no matter what I'm going through or feeling. Thank You for Your joy, Lord. Thank You for Your Word that is a bright light in my life.

MORNING

CHILDREN OF THE RESURRECTION

Neither can they die any more: for they are. . .the children of God, being the children of the resurrection.

LUKE 20:36 KJV

Because I'm Your child, Father God, I don't need to be afraid of death. Jesus conquered death when He rose from the grave, and You promise to save me from eternal death too. When my life here on earth ends, I will live forever with You in heaven! Help me be bold in sharing the good news.

EVENING

WORDS TO LIVE BY

Study this Book of Instruction continually. Meditate on it day and night so you will be sure to obey everything written in it. Only then will you prosper and succeed in all you do.

JOSHUA 1:8 NLT

Father, I respect Your Word. I want to give it first place in my life. The Bible is like my umpire, sorting out problems and answering questions that come up every day. Help me remember that when my actions spring from Your Word, things go well.

DAY 17

MORNING

FOR RAINY DAYS

My voice You shall hear in the morning, O LORD; in the morning I will direct it to You, and I will look up.

PSALM 5:3 NKJV

Lord, it's so dark this morning. I don't want to be in this gray light. I just want to be where You are. I want to be with You, walking on streets of gold. I can't wait for endless days of glory in heaven. Lord, please shine Your love and light on my heart today.

EVENING

PEACE

Grace and peace to you from God the Father.

2 THESSALONIANS 1:2 NIV

Thank You, Father, for Your peace. Help me remember that Your peace is the only true rest for my soul—and that I should always run to You and not an idol in my life. When troubles come my way, please give me an extra dose of Your peace. And when I see others who are upset, help me say or do something that will encourage them to seek out Your peace.

MORNING

WAITING ON GOD

LORD, I wait for you; you will answer, Lord my God.
PSALM 38:15 NIV

I feel like I'm standing at a starting line, Lord, ready to run. All I need is Your signal for me to go. I think I've figured out what I need to do in this situation and I'm ready to do it, but I know I need to wait for Your timing. Help me be patient. Show me when and how to follow Your plan for me.

EVENING

OUR REAL CALLING

We told you with strong words that you should live to please God. He is the One Who chose you to come into His holy nation and to share His shining-greatness.
1 THESSALONIANS 2:11–12 NLV

Lord, whatever job I have when I'm an adult, I know my true calling is pleasing You. You chose me! And now I want to live in a way that both shows my thanks to You and shows other people who You are. Amen.

MORNING

TWENTY-FOUR HOURS

This is the day that the Lord has made.
Let us be full of joy and be glad in it.
PSALM 118:24 NLV

I thank You for this day, Lord, with its twenty-four hours. Only twenty-four. Seems like I always cram so much into my day and then fall into bed exhausted each night. But how many hours do I give to You? Sometimes not even one! Help me give You more of each day, Lord, so we can be closer than ever.

EVENING

FULL OF GOD'S TRUTH

Let the teaching of Christ and His words keep on living in you. These make your lives rich and full of wisdom. Keep on teaching and helping each other. Sing. . .with hearts full of thanks to God.
COLOSSIANS 3:16 NLV

Lord, fill my heart and mind with the words of the Bible, and help me share what I've learned with others so their lives can be rich too and so we all can sing to You with thankful hearts.

MORNING

WHAT PLEASES GOD

[Christ] gave Himself as a perfect gift to God through the Spirit that lives forever. Now your heart can be free from the guilty feeling of doing work that is worth nothing. Now you can work for the living God.

HEBREWS 9:14 NLV

Father God, thank You for forgiving me for my sins and mistakes. Show me the things I do that please You. I want to keep doing those things, even when it's hard. With Your help, I know I can.

EVENING

FALLING

Give all your cares to the Lord and He will give you strength. He will never let those who are right with Him be shaken.

PSALM 55:22 NLV

Lord, it's been a tough day. I'm worried about so much; it's exhausting. So I'm going to follow Your advice and give my cares to You—every last one. Tonight I'm falling into Your arms for the comfort and strength I need. I know You will take care of both my worries and me.

DAY 21

MORNING

SPIRIT-LED

For those who are led by the Spirit
of God are the children of God.

ROMANS 8:14 NIV

Heavenly Father, let Your Spirit lead me in everything. Let me always look to You for guidance. Keep me from the temptation to listen to what the world says I should be or do. Forgive me when I ignore Your Spirit. Help me tune in to Your Holy Spirit so that I hear Your voice every day in each decision and each action.

EVENING

LIVE WORTHY

As a prisoner for the Lord, then, I urge you to live
a life worthy of the calling you have received.

EPHESIANS 4:1 NIV

Lord, I'm not locked in jail like the apostle Paul was, but I'm enslaved by my love for You—a really great thing! You've called me to believe in You, and I take that call seriously. I want to live a life worthy of my calling, like the Bible says. Thank You for helping me. (I know You will!)

MORNING

JUST WANT TO PRAISE

"Then you will have joy in the All-powerful, and lift up your face to God."
JOB 22:26 NLV

Father God, today I just want to praise You! You are awesome; You are holy; You are merciful. You saved me! You are all that is good, Lord, and You are almighty. You made mountains. And trees that reach into the sky and birds as bright as rainbows and flowers so perfect and beautiful. Who is like You? No one compares to You. Amen and amen and amen!

EVENING

HAPPY IS SHE

Where there is no understanding of the Word of the Lord, the people do whatever they want to, but happy is he who keeps the law.
PROVERBS 29:18 NLV

Lord, we'd be lost if we didn't have the Bible to show us how to live. But when we obey You, You work through us to bring Your good plans to completion. I can trust You whether things around me are going smoothly or not. Keeping Your commands and walking in Your blessings make me very happy!

DAY 23

MORNING

THE DAY OF SMALL THINGS

For who hath despised the day of small things? for they shall rejoice.
ZECHARIAH 4:10 KJV

Dear Lord, help me be thankful for the small things. I want to see each day as a chance to celebrate all good things, no matter how small. Thank You for moments that remind me that ordinary days are really extraordinary, because You're a part of them. Thank You for everything You've already given me and everything that's headed my way.

EVENING

IT WAS HIS PLAN

God saved us and called us to live a holy life. He did this, not because we deserved it, but because that was his plan from before the beginning of time— to show us his grace through Christ Jesus.
2 TIMOTHY 1:9 NLT

Lord God, Your plan to save us wasn't random. You set it in motion from the very beginning! And I'm so thankful that it depends not on us but rather on Your grace. Use me to bring other people to You.

MORNING

EXPECTING MIRACLES

Then the fire of the LORD fell and consumed the burnt sacrifice, and the wood and the stones and the dust, and it licked up the water that was in the trench.

1 KINGS 18:38 NKJV

Dear God, I'm praying today knowing You are a miracle-working God. You turned night into day and rolled up the ocean like a scroll. You sent down fire from heaven. You brought the dead back to life. Please answer my prayer today. Work my small miracle.

EVENING

SHARING CHALLENGES

Be an example to all believers in what you say, in the way you live, in your love, your faith, and your purity.

1 TIMOTHY 4:12 NLT

Father God, You know everything I've been through and all the ways I struggle. Help my life be an example to anyone who is going through the same things or struggling in the same ways. I want to share how I've trusted You in my challenges. Give me words to encourage them to trust You too.

DAY 25

MORNING

EVERLASTING WORD

O LORD, You are my God. I will exalt You, I will praise Your name, for You have done wonderful things; Your counsels of old are faithfulness and truth.

ISAIAH 25:1 NKJV

Dear God, the Bible is thousands of years old. How many books made that long ago are still useful today? I can't think of even one! Your Word is as true and helpful today as it was when the ink was wet. I'm so amazed and so thankful. Amen.

EVENING

LIVE WHAT YOU BELIEVE

Let the Holy Spirit lead you in each step. Then you will not please your sinful old selves.

GALATIANS 5:16 NLV

Lord, forgive me when my choices don't line up with what I believe. Teach me Your ways and help me understand Your instructions. I want my faith to affect every area of my life whether I'm at school or home or church. Pull me back when I'm tempted to pull away. Help me be faithful to You always.

MORNING

PEACEMAKERS

Blessed are the peacemakers: for they shall be called the children of God.

MATTHEW 5:9 KJV

Lord, if I want other people to see me as Your child, then I need to try to create peace in my world. Help me say no to stirring up anger or bitterness among my friends and family members. Take away spiteful words that bubble up inside me when I'm mad. Teach me to be kind instead. Teach me to treat people like You would.

EVENING

CREATED FOR GOOD WORKS

We are God's masterpiece. He has created us anew in Christ Jesus, so we can do the good things he planned for us long ago.

EPHESIANS 2:10 NLT

Father God, You shaped me into the unique person I am today. You created me to do good works. Long, long ago, before I was born, You planned the things I would do for You. Give me the courage to do those things. Help me be brave even when the tasks are challenging.

DAY 27

MORNING

THE WATCHER

The LORD will keep you from all harm—he will watch over your life; the LORD will watch over your coming and going both now and forevermore.

PSALM 121:7–8 NIV

Lord, sometimes I feel scared. I'm scared that someone I love will get sick. I'm scared of being alone. I'm scared that I'll make mistakes in life. But as crazy as it sounds, thank You for that fear, Lord—because it encourages me to pray! Thank You for watching over me.

EVENING

SERVING FROM THE HEART

As slaves of Christ, do the will of God with all your heart.

EPHESIANS 6:6 NLT

Lord, I want to do Your will with all my heart and talent. I want to be a girl You can use to help other people. And I don't want to drag my feet—I want to be energetic about it! Help me focus on You and not on the talents You've given me. Help me understand what You've shaped me to do.

MORNING

LOVING ENEMIES

"Love your enemies! Do good to them. Lend to them without expecting to be repaid. Then your reward from heaven will be very great, and you will truly be acting as children of the Most High."

LUKE 6:35 NLT

Dear God, I have a hard time loving some of the people in my life. But You ask me to be kind to my enemies—to do good things for them without thinking about what I'll get back. Not easy! Please help me obey.

EVENING

AUTHENTICITY

"These people honor me with their lips, but their hearts are far from me."

MATTHEW 15:8 NIV

Lord, I want my heart and my actions to line up. The things I do shouldn't be for attention or praise. Please open my eyes to my real motivation when I decide to do something. Keep me honest with myself and You. Remind me that I represent You in the choices I make. In everything, help me honor You from my heart.

DAY 29

MORNING

THE DEAD WILL LIVE!

But your dead will live, LORD; their bodies will rise—
let those who dwell in the dust wake up and shout for joy.
ISAIAH 26:19 NIV

Lord, I feel so sad this morning. I'm missing someone who has died. Death seems so strange and wrong. Thank You for reassuring me that it *is* wrong, that death was not part of Your plan. And that, ultimately, death will be swallowed up in Your victory. We will *live forever* with You. Amen!

EVENING

FORGIVE EACH OTHER

Get rid of all bitterness, rage and anger, brawling
and slander, along with every form of malice.
EPHESIANS 4:31 NIV

Lord, forgiveness can be so hard sometimes. I need Your help to get rid of bitterness and anger. Help me build others up instead of putting them down—even when it seems like they deserve it. Teach me grace. Help me to forgive other people quickly and to be kind and compassionate, because I know Christ forgave all of us.

MORNING

CONSTANT PRAISE

Be full of joy all the time. Never stop praying.
1 THESSALONIANS 5:16–17 NLV

Lord, You've given me life, and I praise You. You've filled my lungs with air from my very first breath, and I praise You. I praise You because I am fearfully and wonderfully made. Today, Lord, I want to pray to You like I breathe: in and out, all day long. Fill my mouth with words that praise You. Let my lips shout how great You are.

EVENING

OBEDIENCE LEADS TO JOY

"If you keep my commands, you will remain in my love, just as I have kept my Father's commands and remain in his love."
JOHN 15:10 NIV

Lord, Your Word says that if we obey Your commands, we will remain in Your love. I want to serve You from an obedient heart. Just as Jesus submits to You, Father, I choose to submit to You too. Empower me, encourage me. Help me want to make decisions that lead to joy.

DAY 31

MORNING

NO RECORD OF WRONGS

[Love] does not demand its own way. It is not irritable, and it keeps no record of being wronged.

1 CORINTHIANS 13:5 NLT

I can't seem to help myself, Lord. I have this list in my mind of all the things people have done to hurt me. I can't seem to let it go. Help me give up keeping score. Help me not to bring up the past over and over but rather to let love erase all these wrongs.

EVENING

GOD'S OFFSPRING

For in him we live, and move, and have our being. . . . For we are also his offspring.

ACTS 17:28 KJV

The world tells me to be independent, to stand on my own two feet. But the truth is that I'm connected to You, the Lord of the universe, and I rely on You for my life. I wouldn't exist if it weren't for You! What a relief that it's not all on me to handle everything.

MORNING

CALL TO ME

"Call to me and I will answer you and tell you great and unsearchable things you do not know."

JEREMIAH 33:3 NIV

Father God, You know everything. You see everything. You are everywhere all the time. Sometimes we think we are so smart. Compared to You, though, we are babies one minute old, not understanding *anything*. You want us to grow up. You want to teach us what You know. So here I am, giving You my mind, Lord. Amen.

EVENING

WHO KNOWS?

Dear friends, now we are children of God, and what we will be has not yet been made known.

1 JOHN 3:2 NIV

Father, I'm grateful to be Your child in this life. I can't even imagine what that will mean in the life to come! Thank You for hope today and hope for my future. Although I don't know all the details of what You have planned, I'm thankful I can know that You have it all under control.

DAY 33

MORNING

JOYFUL LIFE

You will go out with joy, and be led out in peace.

ISAIAH 55:12 NLV

Lord, thank You for the joy You bring to my life. Joy is with me because You are with me! May all creation—even the trees—praise You as I praise You. Help me live with a light heart and a positive attitude, despite the distractions and responsibilities that try to bring me down. I choose You. I choose to go through each day with joy.

EVENING

FILLED WITH JOY

The LORD has done great things for us,
and we are filled with joy.

PSALM 126:3 NIV

Lord, draw me closer to You. In Your presence is joy—and I want to be filled with it! Knowing I am loved by You makes me glad. I can't imagine life without You! Apart from You, people live in darkness, but Your presence brings beautiful, brilliant light. You care; You comfort; You really listen. With You beside me, I am loved and overflowing with joy.

MORNING

THE JOY OF KNOWING JESUS

But let all who take refuge in you be glad; let them ever sing for joy. Spread your protection over them, that those who love your name may rejoice in you.

PSALM 5:11 NIV

Jesus, knowing You equals joy! I can smile because I know You love me. I can be positive because I know You have the power to change things. Being near You makes me so very happy—a fact I want to share with everyone!

EVENING

MAKE ME WISER

If any of you lacks wisdom, you should ask God, who gives generously to all without finding fault, and it will be given to you.

JAMES 1:5 NIV

Father God, I found myself in a tricky situation today. I want to do Your will, but first I need Your wisdom. I'm not Solomon—the wisest man who ever lived—but just like he did, I'm asking for Your wisdom. Thank You that You promise to give it to me generously.

DAY 35

MORNING

EYES ON THE PRIZE

My eyes are on the crown. I want to win the race and get the crown of God's call from heaven through Christ Jesus.

PHILIPPIANS 3:14 NLV

Father God, so many distractions fight for my attention—my phone, clothes, sports—but I want to use my time and energy wisely. The most important thing in my life is knowing You and living for You. I need Your help here, Lord. I can't keep my eyes on the crown, like this verse says, without You!

EVENING

A THANKFUL HEART

Rejoice always, pray continually, give thanks in all circumstances; for this is God's will for you in Christ Jesus.

1 THESSALONIANS 5:16–18 NIV

Lord, You are my God, and I'm glad to give You the deepest part of me: my heart. Transform my heart so it's a joyful, thankful one. I want to be a girl who prays and makes a difference in her world. Lord, today, right where I am, I say thank You!

MORNING

GOD IS LOVE

God is love. Whoever lives in love lives in God, and God in them.
1 JOHN 4:16 NIV

Dear God, You are love—patient, kind, not envious, not proud, not rude, not self-seeking, not easily angered. You keep no record of wrongs. You're not happy about evil, but You rejoice in the truth. You always protect, trust, hope, and keep going. Your love will always remain. It is the greatest thing there is! May I always make my home in Your love.

EVENING

YOU DON'T HAVE TO BE PERFECT

For the law was given through Moses; grace and truth came through Jesus Christ.
JOHN 1:17 NIV

Lord, when I struggle with perfectionism, help me break free! I know wanting things to be done right can be a good thing, but it can go too far. I want to live in Your grace. Keep me from judging myself too harshly and from fearing how others judge me. Help me see that because of Your grace, I am good enough.

DAY 37

MORNING

SHARING THE GOOD NEWS

For I am not ashamed of the gospel of Christ, for it is the power of God to salvation for everyone who believes.

ROMANS 1:16 NKJV

Dear Father God, I'm not always patient about waiting for things. But You are patient, Lord. You are waiting. You are waiting for *us*. You won't return until everyone has had a chance to hear the gospel. Who can I tell, Lord? Who is near me who hasn't heard or understood the good news?

EVENING

DEALING WITH PRIDE

Do not think of yourself more highly than you ought, but rather think of yourself with sober judgment, in accordance with the faith God has distributed to each of you.

ROMANS 12:3 NIV

Lord, help me not to be prideful or arrogant; but when I am, please forgive me. Humble me, Lord, and lift me up so I'm a willing servant. With my eyes on You, not on myself, may I see the needs that other people have and help them.

MORNING

WISDOM AND MIGHT

Blessed be the name of God for ever and ever: for wisdom and might are his.

DANIEL 2:20 KJV

Lord, You are wise. I'll never grasp the vastness of Your knowledge and insight, but I'm thankful to have Your wisdom in my corner. Scripture says that along with being wise, You are powerful too. No matter how strong and mighty we humans think we are, You are the one who has *all* the power. Today I'm relying on Your wisdom and might.

EVENING

SIT DOWN AND REST

Do you not know? Have you not heard? The LORD is the everlasting God, the Creator of the ends of the earth. He will not grow tired or weary.

ISAIAH 40:28 NIV

Lord, I'm so amazed by You, especially by the fact that You never grow tired. I do get tired. I need a break right now! As I sit with You tonight when everything is quiet, help me be still. Help me rest well so that tomorrow I am strong again.

DAY 39

MORNING

THE CHEERLEADER

I can do all things through Christ who strengthens me.

PHILIPPIANS 4:13 NKJV

Dear Lord, in this verse I can hear You cheering me on. What can I do? *All things!* Who's going to help me? *Christ!* What's He going to do? *Strengthen me!* I thank You for bringing these particular words to me right now. I know I'm going to need this verse today, Lord. Help me repeat it in my heart all day long. Amen.

EVENING

CONFIDENCE

The LORD will be at your side and will keep your foot from being snared.

PROVERBS 3:26 NIV

Lord, help me have more confidence—not in myself but in You. I don't want to be arrogant, but I don't want to be a doormat either. Give me a teachable heart. You have so much to show me, and I want to learn Your ways. Learning and growing, I am alive! Full of Your Spirit, I can stand confident and strong.

MORNING

THE GOD OF HOSTS

For behold, He who forms mountains, and creates the wind, who declares to man what his thought is, and makes the morning darkness, who treads the high places of the earth—the LORD God of hosts is His name.

AMOS 4:13 NKJV

Creator God, You formed the mountains and the wind. You control day and night. You lead all the hosts of heaven. . . . Don't let me ever take for granted Your limitless creativity or forget who You are.

EVENING

A PERSON OF WISDOM

Blessed are those who find wisdom, those who gain understanding, for she is more profitable than silver and yields better returns than gold.

PROVERBS 3:13–14 NIV

Lord, I want to be a person of wisdom, not foolishness, because wisdom is what enriches my life. Help me make right choices and behave in a way that is worthy of Your name. I pray that I would be honest and upright every day so my actions reflect You and Your ways.

MORNING

THE CONSTRUCTION SITE

Being confident of this, that he who began a good work in you will carry it on to completion until the day of Christ Jesus.

PHILIPPIANS 1:6 NIV

Father God, I'm a work in progress. Sometimes I feel like there should be construction tape around my rough edges. I'm not who I want to be, and I'm not who You want me to be yet. You love me anyway. Thank You for the sure promise that You are working in me.

EVENING

A LIFE OF LOVE

"Love your neighbor as yourself."

MATTHEW 22:39 NIV

Lord, I want to live a life of love! Show me what true love is—Your love—so I can receive it and give it away to others. Teach me to care for my neighbor as I would care for myself. Let love be my motivation. Help me speak kind, encouraging words and bless others with my actions. I thank You for Your amazing, unconditional, steadfast love for me.

MORNING

WORRIES INTO PRAYERS

Instead of worrying, pray. Let petitions and praises shape your worries into prayers, letting God know your concerns.
PHILIPPIANS 4:6 MSG

Lord God, I praise You for how You are changing me. I praise You for how You are teaching me to pray about my worries. I trust You. *You* are the overcomer; *You* are my resting place; *You* are my strength and my fortress. I am so relieved to give my worries to You and let them become prayers.

EVENING

PRIORITIZE PRAYER

"Blessed is the one who trusts in the LORD, whose confidence is in him."
JEREMIAH 17:7 NIV

Lord, I feel like a withered plant with dry, brown leaves. Help me connect with You in prayer so I can grow strong and healthy, inside and out, like a vibrant green tree. You are my source of living water. Teach me to be still, to listen, to absorb what You want to reveal to me as we talk one-on-one.

DAY 43

MORNING

ANYTHING CAN HAPPEN

Jesus said, "If? There are no 'ifs' among believers. Anything can happen."
MARK 9:23 MSG

Father God, You are so amazing! When You first saved me, I felt like the world had shifted under me and anything was possible. The knowledge that You did miracles (and might for me too) made me feel like I was beginning a new kind of life that would be beautiful and grand. It's not just a feeling, Lord. *Anything* can happen. I praise You for this truth!

EVENING

WHO YOU ARE

God wants these great riches of the hidden truth to be made known to the people who are not Jews. The secret is this: Christ in you brings hope of all the great things to come.
COLOSSIANS 1:27 NLV

Dear Jesus, help me find my identity in You, not the world. As I read the Bible, help me understand who You created me to be. Point out the true identity that is mine through my relationship with You.

MORNING

MAGNIFYING GLASS

O magnify the LORD with me,
and let us exalt his name together.
PSALM 34:3 KJV

Remind me, Lord, that I'm called to be Your magnifying glass. Shine Your light through me to all the world around me. Move me out of the way so that You are the only one others see. My aim is to exalt Your name in everything I do—in my thoughts and my words and my actions—so that my life worships You and only You.

EVENING

I AM GOD'S CHILD

The Spirit of God, who raised
Jesus from the dead, lives in you.
ROMANS 8:11 NLT

Dear Jesus, thank You for providing the way for me to belong to Your family. I am a child of God, and You are my elder brother and my example. I will do my best to follow in Your footsteps. I want to be like You, Lord. I want to have the same character. Thank You for including me in the greatest family ever!

MORNING

OUR REDEEMER

As for our redeemer, the LORD of hosts is his name, the Holy One of Israel.

ISAIAH 47:4 KJV

You are my Redeemer, Lord—You've saved me from all that separated me from You. When I mess up or go my own way, You draw me back and clean me up. When I feel trapped in anxiety or despair, You free me. When I see no way out, You rescue me. When I feel unworthy and beyond all hope of saving, You cover me with grace. I worship You, Lord. Amen.

EVENING

GOD BLESS MY HOME

The LORD's curse is on the house of the wicked, but he blesses the home of the righteous.

PROVERBS 3:33 NIV

Lord, please bless my home. I ask for Your protection to be here with me and my family. Fill each room with Your presence, Your peace, and Your power. May my whole family treat each other with respect and kindness. Use this house in ways that glorify You, Lord. And may anyone who comes here feel at home.

DAY 46

MORNING

GOD SHEPHERDS HIS FLOCK

He tends his flock like a shepherd: he gathers the lambs in his arms and carries them close to his heart.

ISAIAH 40:11 NIV

Lord, I have a friend who's hurting. She needs someone right now, and I'm not sure I can be that someone. I know You care for us like a shepherd taking care of his flock of sheep. Please gather my friend in Your arms, and carry her until she's not hurting anymore.

EVENING

FLOWING WITH THE SEASONS

To everything there is a season, a time for every purpose under heaven.

ECCLESIASTES 3:1 NKJV

Lord God, I know there is a season for everything. The Bible tells me there is a time for every purpose under heaven—a time to weep, a time to laugh, a time to mourn, and a time to dance. Help me recognize the season I'm in and flow with it. Show me how to bend as You lead the way.

DAY 47

MORNING

THE GOD WHO SAVES

O God Who saves us, help us for the honor of Your name. Take us out of trouble and forgive our sins, for the honor of Your name.

PSALM 79:9 NLV

God, You are the only one who can save me and keep me safe forever. No one else—not even the people who love me—can do that. If I start to trust in other people or things when I'm stressed and insecure, point me back to You—the God who saves.

EVENING

ENCOURAGING WORDS

Gracious words are a honeycomb, sweet to the soul and healing to the bones.

PROVERBS 16:24 NIV

Lord, I pray that I would speak encouraging and kind words to my friends and family. Help me build others up—never tear them down. Help me not be so self-absorbed that I forget to ask how others around me are doing. May my words be positive. May they be sweet to the soul and healing to the bones—like honey!

MORNING

WHO ARE MY ENEMIES?

"The LORD will cause your enemies who rise against you to be defeated before your face; they shall come out against you one way and flee before you seven ways."
DEUTERONOMY 28:7 NKJV

I'm not a warrior, Lord, but I do have enemies. Enemies like anger, discontent, pride, selfishness, and laziness. Strengthen me to fight these foes, Lord. I submit to You as my commander. Empower me through Your Spirit so I'll be able to resist my enemies and follow only You.

EVENING

PLANNING AHEAD

Ants—they aren't strong, but they store up food all summer.
PROVERBS 30:25 NLT

Lord, my life gets so busy, sometimes all I can see is today. Remind me to lift my head and look up once in a while. I'm young, but I still want to think about what You might have in store for my future. Help me to set worthy goals and to fix my eyes on You so I can see where we're going together and the plans You have for me.

DAY 49

MORNING

AN ACT OF LOVE

Jesus answered, "Unless I wash you, you have no part with me."

JOHN 13:8 NIV

Lord, I'm thinking about foot washing. The idea of having someone—especially *You*—wash my feet makes me squirm. Foot washing is an act of love, but it's nothing compared to the act of love You showed when You died on the cross. I can never thank You enough for Your sacrifice for me! Help me run to You whenever anything in my life needs to be cleaned up.

EVENING

A HABIT OF SELFLESSNESS

Since Christ has suffered in His body, we must be ready to suffer also. Suffering puts an end to sin.

1 PETER 4:1 NLV

Jesus, I've been self-centered. Sometimes I've felt like the world revolved around me. Forgive me for my selfishness. I won't die if everything doesn't go my way. Help me not to react so emotionally when things don't turn out as I expected them to. Help me think of others before myself, just as You thought about us.

MORNING

GROANING

The Spirit helps us in our weakness. We do not know what we ought to pray for, but the Spirit himself intercedes for us through wordless groans.

ROMANS 8:26 NIV

Lord God, my mind feels empty. I don't know how or what to pray. It seems like a big weight is sitting on my chest, and I'm afraid the only thing that will come out is a horrible noise. Thank You so much for Your Holy Spirit, who speaks for me when I can't.

EVENING

LOOKING FORWARD

"When the Spirit of truth comes, he will guide you into all truth. . . . He will tell you about the future."

JOHN 16:13 NLT

Sometimes I look back at the things that didn't turn out quite right for me, Lord. I know I shouldn't focus on the past. You've set a great life ahead of me, and I want to embrace it wholeheartedly. Help me see the future with joy because my hope is in *You*!

DAY 51

MORNING

WHY I SERVE

"For the LORD *searches all hearts and understands all the intent of the thoughts. If you seek Him, He will be found by you."*

1 CHRONICLES 28:9 NKJV

Lord, we talk a lot about serving others at church. I like to volunteer, but sometimes I'm not sure if I'm serving because I want to help people or because I want to feel good about myself. Search my heart and show me why I serve. Help me serve You and others with the right spirit.

EVENING

SHARING MY BLESSINGS

"All must give as they are able, according to the blessings given to them by the LORD *your God."*

DEUTERONOMY 16:17 NLT

Lord, You have blessed me in a lot of ways. I'm so grateful. And the great thing is that as You bless me, I'm able to bless others. I love the feeling of knowing I'm doing kingdom work! Help me give of my talents, my money, and my time—all for You and the people You love.

MORNING

GLORY TO GOD

Give to the LORD the glory he deserves!
Bring your offering and come into his courts.
PSALM 96:8 NLT

Lord, so many people in this world like to glorify themselves—and not just certain celebrities. I see people every day who want attention. Sometimes, Lord, I'm one of them. But the only one who really deserves all glory is You! Help me give You the glory You deserve. I want to shine a light on how wonderful You are.

EVENING

GIVE AND GET

"Bring the tenth part into the store-house, so that there may be food in My house. Test Me in this," says the Lord of All. "See if I will not then open the windows of heaven and pour out good things for you until there is no more need."
MALACHI 3:10 NLV

Father God, I don't give just so I can get something back, but I'm glad that's how You work. When I give generously, You give generously too. Amazing!

DAY 53

MORNING

CHOOSING LIFE

"I call heaven and earth as witnesses today against you, that I have set before you life and death, blessing and cursing; therefore choose life, that both you and your descendants may live."

DEUTERONOMY 30:19 NKJV

Lord, today I choose life—I choose to live in You. Instead of looking at all I don't have, I look at all You've blessed me with. The list is endless. Thank You so much for being my life, today and every day!

EVENING

GET OUT OF JAIL FREE

Whosoever shall call on the name of the LORD shall be delivered.

JOEL 2:32 KJV

Lord God, the world says there's no such thing as a free pass. It says my actions have consequences, and that's true. But when I'm in trouble, it's not up to me to free myself. I'm not stuck or out of luck. All I have to do is call out to You, and You'll deliver me. Thank You for every time You rescue me!

MORNING

MAJESTY AND STRENGTH

And he shall stand and feed in the strength of the LORD, in the majesty of the name of the LORD his God.

MICAH 5:4 KJV

Lord, just looking at all that's going on in the world leaves me feeling powerless. But the Bible says Your name is majesty and strength. Your name is higher and more powerful than anything in the world. Help me tap into Your power. I can do all things when You give me strength!

EVENING

HEAVENLY BLESSINGS

All praise to God, the Father of our Lord Jesus Christ, who has blessed us with every spiritual blessing in the heavenly realms because we are united with Christ.

EPHESIANS 1:3 NLT

Father God, thank You that because I'm one with Jesus, You've blessed me—a lot! You've given me *every* spiritual blessing. Even the bad things I go through don't seem very bad because I know Your blessings outweigh them. And these spiritual blessings are just a taste of what heaven will be like!

DAY 55

MORNING

THE APPLE OF HIS EYE

Keep me as the apple of your eye;
hide me in the shadow of your wings.
PSALM 17:8 NIV

Lord, Your power is unfathomable. I mean, You created the universe just by speaking! But even though You're almighty and amazing, You care about *me*. You protect me like You would protect Your own eye. You hide me under Your wings like a mighty bird shielding its young. Lord, when I'm feeling vulnerable, help me remember this verse.

EVENING

MY JOB

Don't repay evil for evil. . . . Instead, pay them back with a blessing. That is what God has called you to do, and he will grant you his blessing.
1 PETER 3:9 NLT

Lord, You've given me a job: to bless others. It's easy to bless people I care about. It's not so easy to bless people who don't seem to care about me. Help me repay good for evil. I know You'll repay my blessing with Your blessing.

MORNING

SINGING GOD'S NAME

I will praise the name of God with a song, and will magnify him with thanksgiving.

PSALM 69:30 KJV

Father God, please fill me with Your song. Write in my heart a joyful melody that blesses You. Give me words to praise You and words to encourage the people in my life. Put Your peace and beauty into every note. And help me live out that song every second of my day, no matter what's going on around me.

EVENING

LAUGHTER AND JOY

Our mouths were filled with laughter, our tongues with songs of joy.

PSALM 126:2 NIV

Lord God, thank You for laughter. I can't count the times I've laughed with my friends until it hurt, but still we didn't want to stop! Thank You for Your joy that fills me with peace even when things are going wrong. All I have to do is look up—like I'm looking to You, Lord—and I gain a more positive perspective. Please keep infusing my days with laughter and joy.

MORNING

IN QUIETNESS

This is what the Sovereign LORD, the Holy One of Israel, says: "In repentance and rest is your salvation, in quietness and trust is your strength."

ISAIAH 30:15 NIV

Father God, sitting still isn't something I'm good at. If I'm not busy with my friends or school, I'm bouncing around the house. But You want me to sit with You *in quietness* because that's where my strength comes from. Lord, please settle me down so I can just be here with You.

EVENING

PRAISE THE LORD

May the peoples praise you, God; may all the peoples praise you. The land yields its harvest; God, our God, blesses us.

PSALM 67:5–6 NIV

Father God, I bet You love to hear us praise You—not because You're vain, but because You bless us so much. You adore us, Lord! You give us everything we need and so many other things just to make us happy. So please hear me as I acknowledge how great and good You are!

MORNING

A DAILY BLESSING

"May the LORD bless you and protect you. May the LORD smile on you and be gracious to you. May the LORD show you his favor and give you his peace."

NUMBERS 6:24–26 NLT

Lord, may You bless me and keep me from danger. May You smile on me and help me out whenever I need it. May You show me Your favor and give me Your peace. Be with me every second, Lord, because I need You!

EVENING

A GOD OF JUSTICE

"For I, the LORD, love justice. I hate robbery and wrongdoing. I will faithfully reward my people for their suffering."

ISAIAH 61:8 NLT

Lord, injustice abounds in our world. People aren't always treated fairly, and I hate seeing people suffer because of the wrong-doing of others. You hate wrongdoing too, Lord, and You love justice. I could never right all the wrongs I see, but I can count on You to put things right. Thank You for being a God of justice.

MORNING

SOMETHING TO BOAST ABOUT

Each time he said, "My grace is all you need. My power works best in weakness." So now I am glad to boast about my weaknesses, so that the power of Christ can work through me.

2 CORINTHIANS 12:9 NLT

God, usually when I've heard people brag, they've been talking about their strengths: how smart they are, how talented they are. It seems weird to boast about *weaknesses*. But when I'm weak, Your power works through me. And how amazing is that!

EVENING

THE HEALING EDGE

They begged Him that they might touch the bottom of His coat. As many as touched the bottom of His coat were healed.

MATTHEW 14:36 NLV

Lord, You are *so* powerful that just being near You changes things. People could touch even just the edge of Your coat and receive healing because they believed in Your power. I am near You right now in prayer, even though I can't see You. Please heal what needs healing in my life, Lord. Amen.

MORNING

CALLED BY HIS NAME

Your words became a joy to me and the happiness of my heart. For I have been called by Your name, O Lord God of All.

JEREMIAH 15:16 NLV

Father God, not only have You adopted me as Your child, but You also say that Your name is mine. You chased after me. You accepted me. You love me. I don't deserve to be called Yours, but I'm so happy that I am. Now I want my life to make You proud!

EVENING

OBEDIENCE AND BLESSINGS

"You will experience all these blessings if you obey the LORD your God."

DEUTERONOMY 28:2 NLT

I love blessings, Lord. But sometimes I forget that blessings don't just happen. I can't do whatever I want and still expect You to smile and pour out more blessings. Teach me how to obey You from my heart. I love You so much, and doing what You ask shows that I love You. It blesses me even before You bless me for obeying!

DAY 61

MORNING

THE JOY OF THE LORD

Ezra said to them, "Go, eat and drink what you enjoy, and give some to him who has nothing ready. For this day is holy to our Lord. Do not be sad for the joy of the Lord is your strength."

NEHEMIAH 8:10 NLV

Lord, sometimes I drag my feet and huff because there are things I have to do that I don't want to do. But You tell me to be happy! Help me find joy in You.

EVENING

GOD OVER MONEY

"No one can serve two masters. Either you will hate the one and love the other, or you will be devoted to the one and despise the other. You cannot serve both God and money."

MATTHEW 6:24 NIV

Lord, I want stuff—new clothes and a new phone would be nice. So I understand how some adults are obsessed with money. Getting rich means getting whatever you want. But You're my Master. You matter most. Help me serve You—now and all my life.

MORNING

PRAYER WORKS

The earnest prayer of a righteous person has great power and produces wonderful results.

JAMES 5:16 NLT

God, sometimes I feel like giving up on prayer. Does it really do anything? Do I even know what I should be praying for? But the Bible says that my prayers are powerful and that good things will come from them. So please hear my prayers and shape them to Your will. I'll keep praying. I'll keep believing that prayer works.

EVENING

WHAT WEAKNESS?

That's why I take pleasure in my weaknesses, and in the insults, hardships, persecutions, and troubles that I suffer for Christ. For when I am weak, then I am strong.

2 CORINTHIANS 12:10 NLT

Here it is again, Lord: a flip-flopped view of life. When I'm weak, I'm strong. No one in this world is happy about bad things and weaknesses—except for Christians! Father God, I'm glad that *You* make me strong. I'm glad You turn weakness into strength.

DAY 63

MORNING

HOLY LIKE HIM

But God's discipline is always good for us, so that we might share in his holiness.
HEBREWS 12:10 NLT

Father, whenever I think about discipline, I remember being put in time-out as a kid. Or having one of my "privileges" taken away. It never seemed good for me. It seemed like the worst thing ever! So I need Your help to see Your discipline as good. You want to make me more like You! And that's something I want too.

EVENING

LIKE JESUS

We know that God makes all things work together for the good of those who love Him and are chosen to be a part of His plan. God knew from the beginning who would put their trust in Him. So He chose them and made them to be like His Son.
ROMANS 8:28–29 NLV

Lord God, You're working everything out according to Your plan—and I'm a part of that plan! I want to be more and more like Jesus every day.

MORNING

IN A DRY TIME

On the last and greatest day of the festival, Jesus stood and said in a loud voice, "Let anyone who is thirsty come to me and drink. Whoever believes in me, as Scripture has said, rivers of living water will flow from within them."

JOHN 7:37–38 NIV

Lord, I feel blah right now. But I know this dry time won't last forever, because the Bible says I have rivers of living water in me. Please refresh me today.

EVENING

GOD'S STANDARDS

Dear friends, your real home is not here on earth. You are strangers here. I ask you to keep away from all the sinful desires of the flesh. These things fight to get hold of your soul.

1 PETER 2:11 NLV

Lord, You know me really well. You know my struggles. You have the highest standards for the way I should live, and I want to meet them. So I give myself to Your will and ask for Your help.

MORNING

THE MOST BRILLIANT LIGHT

God is light, and in him is no darkness at all.

1 JOHN 1:5 KJV

Father God, You are light. There is no darkness in Your character. Your brilliance is dazzling—brighter than the brightest star and more beautiful than the most impressive constellation in the night sky. You are the source of never-ending illumination! Please shine on me. Please shine *through* me so that others see the darkness that's in this world and run to Your light.

EVENING

DON'T BE DISCOURAGED

They were just trying to intimidate us, imagining that they could discourage us and stop the work. So I continued the work with even greater determination.

NEHEMIAH 6:9 NLT

Lord, people are trying to intimidate me. They're telling me there's no way I can do what You've asked me to do. But I have faith in You. I know I can do whatever You ask. Help me not to let other people discourage me from reaching my goal.

MORNING

MY GOD

The LORD is my rock and my fortress and my deliverer; my God, my strength, in whom I will trust; my shield and the horn of my salvation, my stronghold.

PSALM 18:2 NKJV

You have so many names, Lord: rock, fortress, deliverer, shield, horn of salvation, stronghold. All of them tell me that I can trust You absolutely. All of them tell me that You are in control, that I shouldn't be afraid, that I'm safe with You. You are my God!

EVENING

FEARLESS

Even if an army gathers against me, my heart will not be afraid.

PSALM 27:3 NLV

I remember the story of David, how he faced wild animals and giants and armies. But he was not afraid. I wish I had that kind of faith! Sometimes I get so scared my heart beats a mile a minute. Lord, when I'm afraid, I'll repeat Psalm 27:3 and remember that You are my reason to be fearless. I'll say these words and kiss fear goodbye.

MORNING

NEED SUPPORT?

Paul would not listen to us. So we stopped begging him and said, "May whatever God wants be done."
ACTS 21:14 NLV

God, sometimes people—even other Christians—don't get what You're doing in my life. They think I'm crazy for following You. But I know that when You ask me to do something, I can be bold to do it. Thank You for the support of my church friends who love and pray for me. Thank You for the encouragement You give me too.

EVENING

JESUS' HOME

Jesus replied, "Foxes have dens and birds have nests, but the Son of Man has no place to lay his head."
MATTHEW 8:20 NIV

Father, the Bible says that Jesus didn't have a home of His own. His home was wherever He happened to be on the road when nighttime came. Today it hit me that my home is Jesus' home too. Help me understand how to live so that Jesus will always feel at home with me.

MORNING

GUARANTEED BLESSING

"The LORD will guarantee a blessing on everything you do."
DEUTERONOMY 28:8 NLT

Lord, the Bible says that You actually *guarantee* a blessing on everything I do that lines up with Your will for me! You will be with me always, helping me every second, putting Your stamp of approval on every good thing I do. What an awesome promise! I can start this day knowing You'll guide me. Thank You for blessing me, Lord!

EVENING

WALKING IN THE TRUTH

Lead me in Your truth and teach me. For You are the God Who saves me. I wait for You all day long.
PSALM 25:5 NLV

Father God, show me in the Bible what Your truth is so that I can walk in it. Teach me patience as I wait for You to act in my life. Waiting is not an easy thing for me to do. Please help me trust in Your salvation. Your truth means everything to me.

DAY 69

MORNING

OUT OF SIGHT

Once, on being asked by the Pharisees when the kingdom of God would come, Jesus replied, "The coming of the kingdom of God is not something that can be observed."

LUKE 17:20 NIV

Lord, Your kingdom isn't something I can see with my eyes. Please give me eyes of faith so I know Your kingdom is real—because it is real! Help me talk about Your kingdom with people who haven't heard about it yet. And may Your kingdom come, Lord!

EVENING

OUR HELP

Our help is in the name of the LORD, who made heaven and earth.

PSALM 124:8 NKJV

I don't need to look any further than You, Lord, for help. It is Your name I trust. Your power will help me in every challenge. You know the plan for my life, and You have prepared me to do everything You want me to do. Help me rely on You. Thank You for hearing and answering my prayer.

MORNING

LIVING SACRIFICES

Therefore, I urge you, brothers and sisters, in view of God's mercy, to offer your bodies as a living sacrifice, holy and pleasing to God—this is your true and proper worship.

ROMANS 12:1 NIV

Father God, I worship You with my words, but sometimes that doesn't seem like enough. Thank You for the reminder that I can worship You with my whole body. My life is an offering, a sacrifice, and You are pleased when I live for You.

EVENING

PATIENCE, PLEASE!

We also pray that you will be strengthened with all his glorious power so you will have all the endurance and patience you need.

COLOSSIANS 1:11 NLT

Jesus, I was working on a big project for school today, and my little sister just had to see what I was doing. She got in the way, and I felt so frustrated. You were always so patient with people, Lord, and You still are! I want to be more like You. Please give me more patience next time.

DAY 71

MORNING

GOOD NEWS

Jesus began a tour of the nearby towns and villages, preaching and announcing the Good News about the Kingdom of God.

LUKE 8:1 NLT

Father God, the fact that Jesus died for our sins so we could have a relationship with You is not just good news—it's the best news ever! Jesus shared the good news about Your kingdom, and I want to share it too. Wherever I go today and tomorrow and every day, please give me opportunities—and the courage—to tell people about You.

EVENING

VICTORY GIVER

I do not trust in my bow; I do not count on my sword to save me. You are the one who gives us victory over our enemies; you disgrace those who hate us. O God, we give glory to you all day long.

PSALM 44:6–8 NLT

Lord God, You are on my side—and nothing is as powerful as You! My enemies are different than the psalm writer's were, but I can still say You've saved me. And I praise You!

MORNING

AT MY SIDE

Everyone deserted me. May it not be held against them. But the Lord stood at my side and gave me strength. . . . And I was delivered.

2 TIMOTHY 4:16–17 NIV

Lord, I'm not going to be upset with people for deserting me. All I really need is You. You are my Savior and my deliverer. You are at my side, and I can feel You here. You're so wonderful, Lord! Thank You for never leaving me.

EVENING

"NOT THAT WAY!"

Your ears shall hear a word behind you, saying, "This is the way, walk in it," whenever you turn to the right hand or whenever you turn to the left.

ISAIAH 30:21 NKJV

Father God, You know how I was tempted to send that text today. I was about to gossip, but then Your Spirit spoke to mine. It was like someone standing behind me saying, "Don't hit SEND." Thank You for the warning, Lord. I'm glad I listened!

DAY 73

MORNING

RIGHTEOUSNESS, PEACE, AND JOY

For the kingdom of God is not eating and drinking, but righteousness and peace and joy in the Holy Spirit.

ROMANS 14:17 NKJV

Lord God, Your kingdom isn't built on the things of this world. It's the complete opposite. Righteousness, peace, and joy are heavenly traits, and we humans can't live them out without Your Spirit. Help me to always turn to You for my satisfaction. Help me live in Your realm of righteousness and peace and joy. Amen.

EVENING

BOLD HOPE

"And now, Lord, what do I wait for? My hope is in You."

PSALM 39:7 NKJV

I hope in You, Lord, and what You want to do through me while I'm here on earth. Don't let me drag my feet in fear, but let me run forward—just like David did when he faced Goliath. David knew that You would *always* be with him. Make me bold too, so I can go anywhere with You and take on giants!

MORNING

THE SOWER

And He said, "The kingdom of God is as if a man should scatter seed on the ground."

MARK 4:26 NKJV

Lord, what does this mean: Your kingdom is like a man scattering seed on the ground? Does it mean I can find Your kingdom everywhere, scattered throughout the world by You? Help me see Your kingdom all around me, especially in places I wouldn't expect to see You. Thank You that You never hold back but are always giving.

EVENING

ENCOURAGE ME!

As soon as I pray, you answer me; you encourage me by giving me strength.

PSALM 138:3 NLT

Sometimes I feel like a weakling when it comes to my faith, Lord. I let my doubts and fears overtake me, and then I shrink from the challenges You put in front of me. Lord, I ask You to encourage me. Give me the strength to do what You want me to do. Bring me where You want me to be.

DAY 75

MORNING

IN THE MOMENT

"Be still, and know that I am God."

PSALM 46:10 NIV

Jesus, did You ever hurry? Did You ever kick Your heels into the donkey's side so it would trot faster? I don't think so. Wherever You were was exactly where You wanted to be right then. I want to be like that. Help me slow down and enjoy my life: small stuff and big stuff, even the struggles that are ultimately making me more like You. I am *here*, and so are You.

EVENING

BY FAITH I GO

It was by faith that Abraham obeyed when God called him to leave home and go to another land that God would give him as his inheritance. He went without knowing where he was going.

HEBREWS 11:8 NLT

What Abraham might've given for a map! But that's what faith is all about. Trusting You, God, even when we can't see. Give me that faith. By faith I will obey You. I will go out, not knowing, because I trust You!

DAY 76

MORNING

A MUSTARD SEED

"[The kingdom of God] is like a mustard seed, which is the smallest of all seeds on earth."

MARK 4:31 NIV

Lord, I want Your kingdom to expand, to get bigger and bigger. Plant a seed of faith in my heart. Make my heart a place where faith can grow easily so that what I do for You will be fruitful. Inspire me through Your Spirit so that I'm always ready to be a part of Your plans.

EVENING

GOD LOOKS AT THE HEART

"The LORD does not look at the things people look at. People look at the outward appearance, but the LORD looks at the heart."

1 SAMUEL 16:7 NIV

Lord, there's so much pressure to be pretty! I want to look good, but I'm happy that You look at my heart. You care about my personality and what I believe in more than my appearance. Help me see other people that way too. Help me be beautiful from the inside out.

DAY 77

MORNING

A CHEERFUL HEART

All the days of the oppressed are wretched,
but the cheerful heart has a continual feast.

PROVERBS 15:15 NIV

Lord, I think I woke up on the wrong side of the bed. But I've heard that having a good day is all in how I look at things. So I'm going to choose to be cheerful. I'm going to choose to be positive, whatever happens. And when I feel myself getting grumpy or sad, I'll ask for Your help.

EVENING

GOD-GIVEN DREAMS

Take delight in the LORD, and he will
give you the desires of your heart.

PSALM 37:4 NIV

Lord, You've given me dreams for things I want to happen in my life. I know that not every desire is from You, so teach me how to take delight in You, like this verse says. When I'm close to You and find my happiness in You, I'll always have the desires of my heart. I'll know which dreams are from You to me.

MORNING

AT THE THRONE

So let us come boldly to the throne of our gracious God. There we will receive his mercy, and we will find grace to help us when we need it most.

HEBREWS 4:16 NLT

Father God, I'm a little worried about some things I have to do today—okay, *a lot* worried. I need Your mercy. Help me not to run from my challenges. Give me the grace, strength, energy, talent, and intelligence I need to overcome every challenge.

EVENING

LIKE CHILDREN

"Truly I tell you, anyone who will not receive the kingdom of God like a little child will never enter it."

MARK 10:15 NIV

Jesus, You know how I hate when people treat me like a little kid. But here's one time I won't mind being like a child, because You said that if I don't receive God's kingdom with childlike faith, I'll never receive it. Give me a child's heart. Help me have the simple belief that You want me to have.

DAY 79

MORNING

ALIVE IN HIM

Then our mouth was filled with laughter, and our tongue with singing. Then they said among the nations, "The LORD has done great things for them."

PSALM 126:2 NKJV

Lord, You have filled my mouth with laughter! My tongue sings Your praises! I'm putting Your Word into action. I'm so alive in You this morning. Life can't get any better than this, and it's all because of Your love for me. Thank You, Lord, for making me whole and happy in You!

EVENING

MORE THAN JUST TALK

For the kingdom of God is not in word, but in power.

1 CORINTHIANS 4:20 KJV

Father God, I talk a good game, but sometimes my heart and actions don't follow through. Thank You for the reminder that Your kingdom is powerful. It's not just a bunch of talk. It's real, and it's here on earth right now. You've asked me to help build Your kingdom—please show me how. Show me ways to serve other people every day.

MORNING

KNOWING GOD'S WILL

Do not conform to the pattern of this world,
but be transformed by the renewing of your mind.
Then you will be able to test and approve what
God's will is—his good, pleasing and perfect will.
ROMANS 12:2 NIV

Lord God, transform me! Get me out of the rut of thinking like the world. Renew my mind so I can know Your will. I want to do what makes You happy. Thank You for reassuring me that You will guide me.

EVENING

IN HIS HAND

"Who among all these does not know that the hand
of the Lord has done this? In His hand is the life of
every living thing and the breath of all men."
JOB 12:9–10 NLV

Lord, I like quick fixes. But You don't always work that way. What You've been showing me is to not wait for everything to be "perfect" before I follow You. Help me trust that You hold my life in Your hand.

DAY 81

MORNING

WHO HOLDS THE REINS?

All a person's ways seem pure to them, but motives are weighed by the LORD. Commit to the LORD whatever you do, and he will establish your plans.
PROVERBS 16:2–3 NIV

Lord, I spend so much time trying to control things. I know that's not what You want. I can only control my own responses to the things happening around me. You are the one who controls everything else. Please help me let go of the reins and let You lead me in Your plans.

EVENING

THE GOD WHO CARES

You look over my path and my lying down. You know all my ways very well.
PSALM 139:3 NLV

Lord, thank You that You are the God who cares! You want the best for me, and You're constantly laying out the next steps in my life journey. You're powerful but also gentle and kind. You love giving me dreams—plus the tools I need to reach them. Whatever I'm doing, help me be a girl who trusts You.

MORNING

BLESSED POVERTY

He looked at His followers and said, "Those of you who are poor are happy, because the holy nation of God is yours."
LUKE 6:20 NLV

Lord, who wants to be poor? But because of You, being poor isn't a negative. I can be poor in this world but rich in You because earthly things aren't the important things. I know You'll take care of me here. And even better—You promise me an incredible reward in heaven!

EVENING

GUIDANCE GIVER

I will instruct you and teach you in the way you should go; I will counsel you with my loving eye on you.
PSALM 32:8 NIV

Father God, thank You for guiding me. You teach me the way I should go. You counsel me and watch over me. Help me listen so I can hear Your direction. And when I hear, give me the courage to walk forward, knowing You're always near. You're with me every step I take.

DAY 83

MORNING

FALLING INTO LIGHT

Therefore He says: "Awake, you who sleep, arise from the dead, and Christ will give you light."

EPHESIANS 5:14 NKJV

Lord, thank You again for the Bible and what it teaches me. When I fall to my knees to pray, You lift me up. I fall, Lord, because I'm small and You're great. I am weak—but You are strong! And You give me light and strength as I pray. Makes me wonder: *Why don't I pray all the time?*

EVENING

TRUSTING GOD'S WISDOM

For the LORD gives wisdom; from his mouth come knowledge and understanding.

PROVERBS 2:6 NIV

Lord, what an awesome privilege to be able to talk to You—the wisest, most intelligent Being in the universe. I have direct access, straight to the top. Thank You for giving me direction even when I can't see the way. Knowledge and understanding come from Your mouth. Remind me to ask for Your wisdom and trust it!

MORNING

DEAD AND GONE

Jesus said to him, "Let the dead bury their own dead, but you go and preach the kingdom of God."
LUKE 9:60 NKJV

Father God, help me let go of what happened days ago—even months ago!—and look ahead. Jesus took care of my sin forever. Give me a new focus (my future) so I'm not preoccupied with what is dead and gone (my past). Fill my mind with thoughts of You and what You're asking me to do each day.

EVENING

NOTHING IS TOO HARD FOR GOD

"I am the LORD, the God of all mankind. Is anything too hard for me?"
JEREMIAH 32:27 NIV

Lord, I know what I want to happen, but there are so many obstacles. I need to trust You more. Nothing is too hard for You. You can do anything! Despite the hard things that are going on around me, please bring opportunities to serve You into my life—please make a way. Line up my goals with Your plans, and help me reach them.

DAY 85

MORNING

CLEANED UP

Christ did this so He could set the church apart for Himself. He made it clean by the washing of water with the Word.

EPHESIANS 5:26 NLV

Father God, sometimes my room gets messy. I need to keep my room clean, but there's something else I should keep even cleaner: my soul. Thank You for making us clean—for getting rid of every bad thing in us. Please show me where I need to clean things up, and help me do it.

EVENING

TRUST THE PLANNER

"'For I know the plans I have for you,' says the Lord, 'plans for well-being and not for trouble, to give you a future and a hope.'"

JEREMIAH 29:11 NLV

Lord, I can count on You for a bright future. Help me understand Your plans. As I share my dreams with You, please make them come true—or squash them like clay on a potter's wheel and turn them into something better than I could've imagined. I trust You. Amen.

MORNING

HEALING

"Heal the sick who are there and tell them, 'The kingdom of God has come near to you.'"

LUKE 10:9 NIV

Lord, You can heal people, whether it's their spirits or minds or bodies that are sick. And there's a lot of sickness in this world. Help me tell people about Your healing. And when I *say* that I'm going to pray for someone, remind me to *actually* pray. Come near to those who are sick and heal them, Lord.

EVENING

GOD IS FAITHFUL

The one who calls you is faithful, and he will do it.

1 THESSALONIANS 5:24 NIV

Father God, I'm so glad that You are faithful. No one else is like You. People move away. People stop being friends. And so many things in life are uncertain too. But You are always here, loving me as much as ever. You keep all Your promises—every one of them, all the time—and I thank You!

DAY 87

MORNING

SANCTIFICATION

God's will is for you to be holy.
1 THESSALONIANS 4:3 NLT

Lord God, You want me to be holy. I've heard it called being "sanctified"—fully set apart for You. So I surrender myself to You. I give You my heart, my relationships, my schoolwork, my hobbies, my health—everything! Gently prod me along to continue surrendering every part of my life to You—especially the parts that I try so hard to take back and control on my own.

EVENING

MY DREAMS

He went on a little farther and got down with His face on the ground. He prayed, "My Father, if it can be done, take away what is before Me. Even so, not what I want but what You want."
MATTHEW 26:39 NLV

Lord, I bow before You and give You my dreams. I yield to Your will. When I'm tempted to do things my way, may I ask for Your guidance instead and trust You. You have everything covered.

MORNING

GIVE THANKS

In every thing give thanks: for this is the will of God.
1 THESSALONIANS 5:18 KJV

Father God, I thank You for all You've given me. Thank You for a body that's healthy. Thank You for food that tastes good and is good for me. Thank You for clothes that keep me warm and look cute too. Thank You for my family and friends (even when they're annoying). And thank You for Jesus, who saved me. Keep my heart overflowing with thanks, Lord!

EVENING

TO KNOW YOU, LORD

"I want you to show love, not offer sacrifices. I want you to know me more than I want burnt offerings."
HOSEA 6:6 NLT

Lord, I want to know You more than I do right now. Help me understand who You are and what You are like. Teach me the things that are important to You so they can become important to me. And help me get rid of distractions that keep me too busy for You. Amen.

DAY 89

MORNING

WORDS, WORDS, WORDS

As new babies want milk, you should want to drink the pure milk which is God's Word. . . . If you have tasted of the Lord, you know how good He is.

1 PETER 2:2–3 NLV

Lord, it seems like everybody has something to say. But not all that I hear glorifies You. Help me filter out what isn't good. Help me want to drink up only Your pure words so that they're what comes out when I speak.

EVENING

KNOWING THE TRUTH

And we know that the Son of God has come, and he has given us understanding so that we can know the true God. And now we live in fellowship with the true God.

1 JOHN 5:20 NLT

Jesus, thank You for coming to this earth so that I can know God the Father and His truth. Truth is the reason You came, and it doesn't change with how I think or feel. Help me know the truth and live it out.

MORNING

MY DELIGHT

I delight to do thy will, O my God.
PSALM 40:8 KJV

Lord, if You were a cruel god, there's no way I could delight in doing Your will. But You are a loving God, and Your will for me isn't sadness and gloom. Your will is good! I'm beyond happy that You love me and that you care for me and do what is best for me. Whenever I hesitate to do what You've asked me to do, remind me that obedience to You is a joy.

EVENING

GODLY EMOTIONS

"The LORD is slow to anger, abounding in love and forgiving sin and rebellion."
NUMBERS 14:18 NIV

Lord, some days I feel all over the place with my emotions. I'm sad. Then I'm happy. Then I'm annoyed. Then I'm happy again. Emotions are good, but I definitely want to be more like You—slow to anger, abounding in love, forgiving. Help me see when I'm overreacting. Help me think, speak, and act in godly ways, whatever happens.

DAY 91

MORNING

HEAL MY BROKEN HEART!

He heals the brokenhearted and bandages their wounds.
PSALM 147:3 NLT

Father God, lately I've been obsessing over certain people who hurt me. Turns out words *can* hurt! And I'm only making it worse by thinking about it and thinking about it and thinking about it. Lord, the Bible says You heal the brokenhearted and bandage their wounds. I need that today. Heal me. Help me pray for the ones who hurt me, because that's part of healing too.

EVENING

LOVE FOR OTHERS

Dear friends, let us love each other, because love comes from God. Those who love are God's children.
1 JOHN 4:7 NLV

Lord, You are the author of love. As I read the Bible, teach me what love really is. You are so good at loving people—You are kind, compassionate, interested, and accepting. You want the best for people. You feel their joy and sadness. You make them feel special. Lord, let me be a person who loves like that.

MORNING

FOREVER

And this world is fading away, along with everything that people crave. But anyone who does what pleases God will live forever.

1 JOHN 2:17 NLT

Father God, thanks for the reminder that the things in this world won't last. I don't know why I get excited about buying stuff. It's a lot of fun, but pretty soon I'm over one thing and thinking about getting something else. Life with You isn't like that—it lasts forever. Help me focus on eternity, Lord. Amen.

EVENING

PATIENCE WHILE WE WAIT

Be patient, then, brothers and sisters, until the Lord's coming. See how the farmer waits for the land to yield its valuable crop, patiently waiting for the autumn and spring rains.

JAMES 5:7 NIV

Lord, have I said this already? It's hard for me to wait! There are things I want. But You give us waiting seasons for a reason. I ask for patience today. Help me understand that You're not just killing time—You're shaping who I'll become.

DAY 93

MORNING

FIRST THINGS FIRST

"Seek the Kingdom of God above all else, and live righteously, and he will give you everything you need."
MATTHEW 6:33 NLT

I know You understand, Lord, that there are important things in my life—like family, school, and my future. It's hard sometimes to realize that these things aren't the *most* important. You promise that when I put You first, You'll take care of my needs. I don't have to worry about every detail, because You're already working everything out.

EVENING

MY CONFIDENCE

Have no fear of sudden disaster or of the ruin that overtakes the wicked, for the LORD will be at your side and will keep your foot from being snared.
PROVERBS 3:25–26 NIV

Lord, I want to be more confident. Please help me to understand that *You* are my confidence. You have the power to make things right even when they go wrong. Let me walk with my head held high because I know I'm Yours!

MORNING

JUST REST

"Come to me, all of you who are weary and carry heavy burdens, and I will give you rest. Take my yoke upon you. Let me teach you, because I am humble and gentle at heart."

MATTHEW 11:28–29 NLT

Lord, I'm so hard on myself. It's exhausting, always trying to be better and better. I'm glad You promise to give me rest. You're not a merciless boss—You walk with me and teach me to do everything You want me to do. Thank You!

EVENING

NEVER SHAKEN

Cast your cares on the LORD and he will sustain you; he will never let the righteous be shaken.

PSALM 55:22 NIV

Lord, when I was a kid, I used to go fishing with my dad. That's what this verse reminds me of—casting my cares away like a line from a fishing rod. Don't let me reel them back in! Take all my worries and give me Your peace instead. Keep me strong and steady, even when I'm stressed.

DAY 95

MORNING

I'M FORGIVEN!

In Him we have redemption through His blood, the forgiveness of sins, according to the riches of His grace.
EPHESIANS 1:7 NKJV

Lord, I pray to You today, thanking You for forgiveness. I'll always be thanking You for forgiveness because it has changed my life. You've cleared my record! In Your mind, it's like I've never sinned. That means I don't have to feel guilty. I can live every day without the weight of past mistakes dragging me down. Thank You! Thank You!

EVENING

MY COMPANION

"Surely I am with you always, to the very end of the age."
MATTHEW 28:20 NIV

Lord, thank You that You're my companion—that I'm never alone. You've assigned angels to watch over and protect me. You've given me Your Holy Spirit and promised that You're with me always, to the end of the world. I'm amazed and thankful that You call me Your friend. Wherever I go, I'll enjoy being with You, Lord. Help me never forget that You're here.

MORNING

KEEP GOING

Patient endurance is what you need now,
so that you will continue to do God's will.
Then you will receive all that he has promised.
HEBREWS 10:36 NLT

God, I want to do Your will. Sometimes, though, I'm impatient and start to doubt the goodness of Your plan for me. I'm distracted by temptations to disobey You—to do my own thing. Deep inside me, I know that wouldn't be good for me. So I'll keep following You, keep trusting You and Your promises.

EVENING

GOODBYE, GUILT

I told my sin to You. I did not hide my
wrong-doing. I said, "I will tell my sins to the
Lord." And You forgave the guilt of my sin.
PSALM 32:5 NLV

Lord, I can't hide my sin from You. You know everything I've done wrong, but You want me to admit it—not so You can condemn me, but so You can make things better! So here goes. I'll confess my wrongs, confident that You'll forgive each one. . .

MORNING

MADE NEW

Therefore, if anyone is in Christ, the new creation has come: The old has gone, the new is here!
2 CORINTHIANS 5:17 NIV

Father God, no matter how healthy we are on the outside, we all have hidden wounds. I've been treated badly in the past, and the damage still hurts. You know my wounds better than I do, Lord. The Bible says that You can make things new. Take away the old, please. Make me new.

EVENING

A NEW SONG

He put a new song in my mouth,
a hymn of praise to our God.
PSALM 40:3 NIV

Lord, I know there's no mess too big for You to clean up, no life too broken for You to fix, and no loss too great for You to make up for it. I know You'll lift me out of this problem eventually. Give me a new song to sing, a happier tune! I praise You, God, for everything You do.

MORNING

MORE THAN ENOUGH

God can give you all you need. He will give you more than enough. You will have everything you need for yourselves. And you will have enough left over to give when there is a need.

2 CORINTHIANS 9:8 NLV

Lord, You've always given me everything I need. Actually, You've given me much more than I need a lot of the time. I never want to forget how good You are. Show me ways that I can share Your blessings with others.

EVENING

GOD'S GREATEST GIFT

For God so loved the world that he gave his one and only Son, that whoever believes in him shall not perish but have eternal life.

JOHN 3:16 NIV

Heavenly Father, thank You for giving the greatest gift ever (Your Son!) so that I can live each day with You. I'll never be able to understand how much it cost You, but I know You did it for me. I'm so thankful Jesus was willing to give His life for mine.

DAY 99

MORNING

GOD'S PROVISION

You open Your hand and satisfy
the desire of every living thing.
PSALM 145:16 NKJV

Lord God, there's no creature on earth You don't see or provide for. I'm praising You right now for the daily gifts You give me. It's through Your goodness that I have food, clothes, and shelter. Help me always be thankful for what I have and not complain. Your power is awesome. Thank You for giving so generously each and every day.

EVENING

TAKING UP MY CROSS

Then he said to the crowd, "If any of you wants to
be my follower, you must give up your own way,
take up your cross daily, and follow me."
LUKE 9:23 NLT

Jesus, following You requires sacrifice. I have so many dreams for my life, but they don't amount to anything unless they include You. Help me let go of the things that aren't meant to be a part of my life. I give You myself—completely!

MORNING

CHOOSING TO REST

In six days the LORD made the heavens and the earth, the sea, and all that is in them, but he rested on the seventh day. Therefore the LORD blessed the Sabbath day and made it holy.

Exodus 20:11 NIV

Lord, You're all-powerful. You don't get tired. But You chose to rest after You created the universe. You set an example for me. I don't like to rest—I'd rather be doing something all the time. Please help me set aside time to rest just like You.

EVENING

ASKING FOR GOD'S HELP

But God is my helper. The Lord keeps me alive!

Psalm 54:4 NLT

Father God, sometimes I think I should work things out on my own. I know I shouldn't feel like I'm bothering You, but my problems seem small compared to other people's. Help me trust the Bible when it says You are my helper. You *want* to help me. So I'm asking—please help. You know what I'm dealing with, and I gladly accept Your help today.

DAY 101

MORNING

GOD'S RICHES

And my God will give you everything you need because of His great riches in Christ Jesus.

PHILIPPIANS 4:19 NLV

Why should I ever doubt Your ability to give me what I need, Lord, when Your riches are so great? I can't even imagine how great Your riches are, and You want to share them with me! Help me remember that everything I call "mine" is actually Yours. Help me use what You give me in ways that honor You and show how thankful I am.

EVENING

ROOTED AND BUILT UP

Just as you received Christ Jesus as Lord, continue to live your lives in him, rooted and built up in him, strengthened in the faith as you were taught, and overflowing with thankfulness.

COLOSSIANS 2:6–7 NIV

Jesus, when You're part of my life—no, when You *are* my life—I'm not some scraggly plant that gets blown over by the wind. I'm rooted. I'm growing. I'm strong! Help me continue to live my life in You.

MORNING

PRAYING FOR OTHERS

The LORD thunders at the head of his army;
his forces are beyond number, and mighty
is the army that obeys his command.

JOEL 2:11 NIV

Lord, I said I'd pray for someone, but then I forgot. (Ugh!) Forgetting to pray is like leaving a wounded soldier behind on the battlefield. Prayer *does* change things. It's powerful because You're powerful. So when You show me people who need me to pray for them, help me obey You.

EVENING

NO WANTS

The LORD is my shepherd; I shall not want.

PSALM 23:1 KJV

Lord, because You're looking out for me—guarding me and guiding me—I have everything I need. You are the good shepherd who takes care of me, Your sheep. I can't see the big picture. I can't see the dangers over the hill or the blessings that are mine to find. So help me trust You absolutely. With You, I'm not lacking a single thing!

DAY 103

MORNING

A HEART TO SEE

I pray that your hearts will be flooded with light so that you can understand the confident hope he has given to those he called—his holy people who are his rich and glorious inheritance.

EPHESIANS 1:18 NLT

Lord, each morning You open the eyes of my heart and flood it with light. I'm filled with hope that will go on forever. I celebrate as I think about what I mean to You and what You, in turn, mean to me.

EVENING

FULLY CHARGED

"God is my strength and power, and He makes my way perfect."

2 SAMUEL 22:33 NKJV

Father God, as I get older, I have more and more responsibilities and sometimes get stressed out. Thanks for the reminder that my help—whatever I need—comes from You. You are my power source. I don't have to go through life alone. You're making my way perfect. You're always here to recharge me when my batteries are running low. Please recharge me for tomorrow, Lord. Amen.

MORNING

A PRAYER FOR GODLY WORDS

The Sovereign LORD has given me his words of wisdom, so that I know how to comfort the weary. Morning by morning he wakens me and opens my understanding to his will.

ISAIAH 50:4 NLT

Lord, here I am this morning, waiting for Your words of wisdom. Please give me direction. Open my eyes and spirit to understand Your will for me. Help me know how to use Your words to comfort other people. Guide me every time I speak.

EVENING

NONE LIKE YOU

"No one is holy like the LORD, for there is none besides You, nor is there any rock like our God."

1 SAMUEL 2:2 NKJV

Lord, You are the one true God. Other so-called deities disappoint their followers, and idols fail. But You never do. Because You're perfect in holiness, all Your other characteristics are only good. There's no selfishness, hate, or dishonesty in You, Lord. I can trust You without a single doubt. What an awesome God You are!

DAY 105

MORNING

RIGHT THERE WITH ME

I will praise the LORD, who counsels me;
even at night my heart instructs me.
PSALM 16:7 NIV

Dear God, sometimes I go to sleep thinking about a problem and then wake up in the morning with the perfect solution. I know those solutions come from You. Thank You for counseling me in the night, for teaching me even when I'm unaware. Even when I don't see Your hand or hear Your voice, You're right there with me.

EVENING

MADE A MISTAKE

Indeed, we all make many mistakes. For if we could control our tongues, we would be perfect and could also control ourselves in every other way.
JAMES 3:2 NLT

Lord, I did it again. I said something I wish I could unsay. Why can't I control my tongue? Is there an easy way to never say what I shouldn't? Give me the courage to admit I've made a mistake and make things right. Please help me do better next time.

MORNING

A LESSON FROM THE BIRDS

"Look at the birds. They do not plant seeds. They do not gather grain. They have no grain buildings for keeping grain. Yet God feeds them. Are you not worth more than the birds?"

LUKE 12:24 NLV

Father God, You keep track of birds, so I know I can trust You to watch over my life. I'm worth a whole lot more to You than any bird. And even though I don't deserve it, I thank You for Your love.

EVENING

MORE THAN CLOTHING

"That is why I tell you not to worry about everyday life—whether you have enough food and drink, or enough clothes to wear. Isn't life more than food, and your body more than clothing?"

MATTHEW 6:25 NLT

Lord, so many things in life are more important than clothes. Sometimes I worry because other girls in my class always have something new to wear and I don't. Turn my eyes to You. Help me see what matters most and not worry.

DAY 107

MORNING

JESUS' WORD POWER

[Jesus said,] "It is the Spirit that gives life. The flesh is of no help. The words I speak to you are spirit and life."

JOHN 6:63 NLV

Jesus, Your words are so powerful, they give life! I may try and try to do good things in my own strength, but my efforts will just fail apart from Your power working inside me. Let Your Spirit speak to mine all day long so I have Your power helping me live and making me alive today.

EVENING

CONTROLLING MY TONGUE

If you claim to be religious but don't control your tongue, you are fooling yourself, and your religion is worthless.

JAMES 1:26 NLT

Lord, never let me forget how important it is for my words and my faith to match. If I say I'm a Christian but people hear me bad-mouth someone or use curse words, then they'll question whether my faith is real. Help me control my tongue. I want my words to shout that I believe in You.

MORNING

THE GOD-BREATHED WORD

All Scripture is God-breathed and is useful for teaching, rebuking, correcting and training in righteousness.

2 TIMOTHY 3:16 NIV

The Bible isn't just a book. It came straight from You, God, through dozens of writers to me—like it was breathed out. "God-breathed" is a great description because Your Word really does give us life, just like the air we breathe. It shows us how to live Your way. Use Your Word to teach me all my life.

EVENING

THREE STEPS

Understand this, my dear brothers and sisters: You must all be quick to listen, slow to speak, and slow to get angry.

JAMES 1:19 NLT

God, dealing with people is hard sometimes. But You've given me three steps that help a lot. Step one: Work on my listening skills. Step two: Pause and pray before I speak. And step three: Get my temper under control. Help me, please. With You, I know I can get this right!

DAY 109

MORNING

PRAYER AND THANKSGIVING

Don't worry about anything; instead, pray about everything. Tell God what you need, and thank him for all he has done.

PHILIPPIANS 4:6 NLT

Even while I'm asking You for something, Lord, I can already thank You. I know You hear my prayers and will answer them. Next time I'm worried, I'll say a prayer. I'll tell You what I need and then be confident that You'll handle it. Thank You for the many ways You've shown up in my life.

EVENING

SAFE IN DANGER

For in the day of trouble he will keep me safe in his dwelling; he will hide me in the shelter of his sacred tent and set me high upon a rock.

PSALM 27:5 NIV

Lord, I need Your protection. Please keep me safe. Hide me away in Your shelter. Comfort me with Your peace and love. Nothing can harm me when You're here next to me. Thank You for enabling me to move from fearful to fearless!

MORNING

DIVERSE GIFTS

There are different kinds of gifts,
but the same Spirit distributes them.

1 CORINTHIANS 12:4 NIV

Father God, last Sunday at church I started thinking about the different gifts people have. Some are teachers. Some are singers. Some pray for people. Some volunteer. . . I don't know exactly what my gift is, but I know You've given me a way to serve You that's uniquely mine. Show me, please. Show me what my part is in Your big family.

EVENING

NEVER ALONE

"I will never leave you nor forsake you."

JOSHUA 1:5 NIV

God, the Bible says You will never leave me, but right now I feel all alone. Some things in my life are making me afraid, and since I can't see You, it seems like I have to face them by myself. Help me know—*really* know—that You are with me. You'll walk beside me every day through everything. Thank You that I never need to be afraid!

DAY 111

MORNING

HE HEARS US

And if we know that he hears us—whatever we ask—
we know that we have what we asked of him.

1 JOHN 5:15 NIV

God, You're always listening to me. You never ignore my prayers, no matter how silly or unimportant I think my words might be. I don't know how You hear every prayer being offered to You at the same time, but You do! And more than that—You answer. I can be sure of it!

EVENING

FREED FROM FEAR

I prayed to the LORD, and he answered
me. He freed me from all my fears.

PSALM 34:4 NLT

Lord, fear is such an awful feeling. I wish there was some way to get rid of all my fear. Oh wait—there is! All I have to do is pray. All I have to do is ask You to take away these fears while I trust You with whatever's happening. It sounds too easy, Lord, but I know it's true.

MORNING

STRONGER

And we know that in all things God works for the good of those who love him, who have been called according to his purpose.

ROMANS 8:28 NIV

Lord, I'm having trouble believing that some of the things happening in my life right now are really making me stronger. They seem to be tearing me down. But I'm going to trust You. I'm going to trust that You're using all these things for my good. And I'm going to look forward to seeing how.

EVENING

NO DOUBT

When you ask, you must believe and not doubt, because the one who doubts is like a wave of the sea, blown and tossed by the wind.

JAMES 1:6 NIV

Father God, I've seen the ocean on a really windy day. The waves swirl and churn turbulently. That's how I feel when I doubt You. I think one thing, then another—until I don't know what I think! When I ask for Your help, Lord, first help me not to doubt.

MORNING

NOT AFRAID

So we say with confidence, "The Lord is my helper; I will not be afraid. What can mere mortals do to me?"

HEBREWS 13:6 NIV

Lord, You are my helper, and I won't be afraid of anything! You shield me from the trouble this world throws at me. Nothing is as powerful as You, and no harm can reach me without first coming through You. I'll say to the whole world, "The Lord is my helper! I'm not afraid!"

EVENING

WHY OBEY?

And whatever we ask we receive from Him, because we keep His commandments and do those things that are pleasing in His sight.

1 JOHN 3:22 NKJV

Father God, I know that the benefits of keeping Your commandments and doing what pleases You go way beyond getting what I ask for. Your commandments are meant to protect me and allow me to live in the freedom that comes with Your love. Lord, please forgive me for the times I've disobeyed.

MORNING

TO EVERY GENERATION

Your faithfulness endures to all generations.
PSALM 119:90 NKJV

Lord God, for thousands and thousands of years, people have testified that You always come through. Sometimes I feel like You overlook me or don't hear my prayers, but I know that's just how I feel. You didn't promise that I would always understand Your ways, but You did promise to be with me and love me always. And You always have. You're as faithful as ever!

EVENING

LEANING ON GOD

For you have been my hope, Sovereign LORD, my confidence since my youth.
PSALM 71:5 NIV

Lord, I'm not very old; but even when I was younger, I remember feeling like I could do anything because of You. You are my confidence. You are the one who makes me strong. Whenever I feel wobbly, I can just lean back on You in my heart and know that You will be there to hold me up. Thank You for being my hope.

DAY 115

MORNING

PERSISTENCE!

"Ask and it will be given to you; seek and you will find; knock and the door will be opened to you."
MATTHEW 7:7 NIV

Father God, I'm going to trust You enough to ask You for what I need—and then to keep asking, seeking, and knocking until You answer. Help me not to grow weary of praying to You about the same thing. I know You'll keep Your promises. I know You hear me and are working out all the details of my life.

EVENING

NO FEAR IN LOVE

There is no fear in love. But perfect love drives out fear, because fear has to do with punishment. The one who fears is not made perfect in love.
1 JOHN 4:18 NIV

Because Your love is unconditional, Lord, there's nothing I could do that would make You stop loving me. My mistakes. My bad attitudes. My failures. All of it was forgiven when I believed in You and received You as my Savior. You love me perfectly. And I can love You back fearlessly!

MORNING

ILLUMINATION

Break open your words, let the light shine out,
let ordinary people see the meaning.
PSALM 119:130 MSG

Father God, I've heard people say that Your Word lights their path. It brightens the darkness in the world so they know where to go and what to do. I want that too, Lord. As I read the Bible, use it like a floodlight in my life so I don't stumble around in the dark. Let Your light shine out! Amen.

EVENING

GOD STRENGTHENS YOU

"Don't be discouraged, for I am your God.
I will strengthen you and help you. I will hold
you up with my victorious right hand."
ISAIAH 41:10 NLT

Lord, I was at a track meet, and one of the runners fell. Her teammate helped her finish the race, the two of them running side by side. That's what You do too. You support me with Your invisible arm around my shoulder. You hold me up so I'm victorious just like You!

DAY 117

MORNING

ANYTHING?

"I tell you, you can pray for anything, and if you believe that you've received it, it will be yours."
MARK 11:24 NLT

Whoa, Lord! This is a huge promise. I can pray for anything, and if I believe, it will be mine? I know "anything" here means anything that aligns with Your will, because You can't be untrue to Yourself. So please help me desire what You desire. Then I'll be able to pray for anything and believe that it's on the way.

EVENING

CHEERFUL GIVING

You must each decide in your heart how much to give. And don't give reluctantly or in response to pressure. "For God loves a person who gives cheerfully."
2 CORINTHIANS 9:7 NLT

Lord, I'm learning that *how much* I give isn't what matters most but rather *how* I give. If I'm giving my money or time or talents just because I feel like I have to, then I'm not giving cheerfully. Change my heart, Lord, so I give out of love just like You do.

MORNING

JESUS LOVES THE LITTLE CHILDREN

And he took the children in his arms, placed his hands on them and blessed them.

MARK 10:16 NIV

Jesus, I'm going to be honest here: Sometimes kids are annoying! My little sister and her friends get in the way and make messes. But You love kids. You hugged them and blessed them when You were on earth. Help me see kids through Your eyes. Help me love them and pray for them and point them to You.

EVENING

WORRY NO MORE

"Therefore I tell you, do not worry. . . . Can any one of you by worrying add a single hour to your life?"

MATTHEW 6:25, 27 NIV

Lord, these verses remind me of something my mom said—that worry doesn't do anything but worry us. Worrying will make us worry more, but we won't have solved anything! You say, "Don't worry," and for good reason: You will take care of us. You promise. And I believe You!

DAY 119

MORNING

TOMORROW

"Give your entire attention to what God is doing right now, and don't get worked up about what may or may not happen tomorrow. God will help you deal with whatever hard things come up when the time comes."

MATTHEW 6:34 MSG

I have no control over tomorrow, Lord. But I can choose to focus on today. I know You'll be with me to help me through whatever tomorrow throws at me—just like You're here helping me right now.

EVENING

THANKFUL FOR FRIENDS

There are "friends" who destroy each other, but a real friend sticks closer than a brother.

PROVERBS 18:24 NLT

Lord, I thank You for my friends, my *real* friends. I'm grateful for the good things they bring into my life. Help me see when a "friend" really isn't a friend and when a relationship might be bad for me. And please help me to be a loyal friend, sticking with my friends no matter what they're going through.

MORNING

MY HEART'S DESIRES

Be happy in the Lord. And He will give you the desires of your heart.
PSALM 37:4 NLV

Thank You, Lord, for creating the deepest, truest desires in me. You've made me unique from everybody else. You've also given me a desire to obey You. The more time I spend with You, the more I know that I'm happiest with You. I'm happiest when I'm following Your will. It's then I can be sure that You'll give me what my heart desires.

EVENING

COME AND HEAR!

Come and hear, all you who fear God; let me tell you what he has done for me.
PSALM 66:16 NIV

Father God, You've done amazing things in people's lives. You've done amazing things in *my* life. Help me tell about those amazing things. But help me be a good listener too. Help me hear Your praises all the time so that the record of Your goodness keeps getting longer and longer in my heart.

MORNING

GONE!

As far as the east is from the west, so far has He removed our transgressions from us.

PSALM 103:12 NKJV

Lord God, I'm so glad You've redeemed my life—You've saved me from what I've done wrong. I'm beyond grateful that You've removed my sins so I have a fresh start. Like someone using a whiteboard, You wiped away the guilt. Father, I know I will never be perfect here on earth, but I also know that I'm forgiven!

EVENING

LOVE ONE ANOTHER

[Jesus said,] "Love one another; as I have loved you."

JOHN 13:34 NKJV

Jesus, You've given us a great example of love—the *greatest* example! You gave Your life for everyone, even when we were sinners and didn't deserve it. Fill me with that kind of love, Lord. I want to be like You. Give me Your power to love those who love me, those who hate me, and those who don't feel one way or the other. Amen.

MORNING

OPEN WIDE!

I am the LORD thy God, which brought thee out of the land of Egypt: open thy mouth wide, and I will fill it.
PSALM 81:10 KJV

Lord, like a baby bird, I'll open wide my soul's mouth, knowing You'll always feed me all I need. Open up my heart today and fill it with just what I need: encouragement, joy, peace, strength, comfort, patience, kindness, love. . . I'm ready, Lord—fill me up!

EVENING

PRAYING FOR THE HURTERS

When Job prayed for his friends,
the LORD restored his fortunes. In fact,
the LORD gave him twice as much as before!
JOB 42:10 NLT

Job prayed for his friends even though they hurt him, and You blessed him, Lord. Sometimes I struggle to overlook the hurtful things people say and do. Help me be more like Job. I want to forgive and forget. I want to love and serve my friends even when they've hurt me.

MORNING

A NEW EARTH

Now I saw a new heaven and a new earth, for the first heaven and the first earth had passed away.

REVELATION 21:1 NKJV

Father God, I wish there weren't diseases in our world. Sickness didn't exist in the Garden of Eden, but it sure is a part of life now. Someday You'll create a new earth, and I know germs won't stand a chance there. I'm looking forward to it, Lord, because then the world will be "very good" again.

EVENING

WAITING ON THE FUTURE

Know also that wisdom is like honey for you: If you find it, there is a future hope for you, and your hope will not be cut off.

PROVERBS 24:14 NIV

Lord, You've made promises about my future. I know everything You've promised will happen, and I'm excited about the future. Help me be wise. Help me be patient, doing what I should be doing now while I'm on my way to the great future You've planned for me.

MORNING

WATERED

The Lord will always lead you. He will meet the needs of your soul in the dry times and give strength to your body. You will be like a garden that has enough water, like a well of water that never dries up.

ISAIAH 58:11 NLV

Lord, sometimes life seems a little boring; other times life is really hard. When things around me are dry and dead and dusty, thank You for watering my soul so that I'm not dry and dead and dusty too.

EVENING

LOVED FOREVER

I am convinced that neither death nor life, neither angels nor demons, neither the present nor the future, nor any powers, neither height nor depth, nor anything else in all creation, will be able to separate us from the love of God that is in Christ Jesus our Lord.

ROMANS 8:38–39 NIV

No matter what happens, Lord, I can't be separated from You and Your love. It's here to stay. You love me always. And I love You right back!

MORNING

HUNGRY SOUL

For he satisfieth the longing soul,
and filleth the hungry soul with goodness.
Psalm 107:9 KJV

Father God, my soul gets so hungry for You sometimes. I know You haven't moved away from me, but rather I've wandered from You. You are immovable, unshakable, always there. I know just where to run to find You. Keep my soul linked with Yours so I'm not tempted to wander away again. Thank You for being patient with me.

EVENING

UNKNOWN FUTURE

Indeed, how can people avoid what
they don't know is going to happen?
Ecclesiastes 8:7 NLT

Dear Lord, I don't know what will happen tomorrow or the next day or any day after that. My mind is filled with what-ifs, and it's driving me crazy! Fill my mind and heart with You instead. I want to be confident in Your power to guide me. Even though You don't tell me everything that's going to happen, You will make me ready for anything.

MORNING

HELP FOR SLEEPYHEADS

It is good to tell of Your loving-kindness in the morning, and of how faithful You are at night.

PSALM 92:2 NLV

Father God, You know I'm not a morning person. I'm not like some of my friends who love getting up early. It's hard for me to wake up and spend time with You every morning. Please energize me, Lord. Keep me motivated and wanting to pray, because I know that drawing close to You brings blessings into my life.

EVENING

DECISIONS, DECISIONS

"I am the LORD your God, who teaches you what is good for you and leads you along the paths you should follow."

ISAIAH 48:17 NLT

Too many choices, Lord! That's what today felt like. I just don't know what I'm supposed to do. So I'm happy to read this verse. I don't have to know instinctively what is good. You promise to teach me and lead me. I'll always know which way to go as long as I'm listening to You.

DAY 127

MORNING

GENERATION TO GENERATION

Know therefore that the LORD your God is God; he is the faithful God, keeping his covenant of love to a thousand generations of those who love him and keep his commandments.

DEUTERONOMY 7:9 NIV

Lord, You have *always* been faithful. Thank You for the men and women in my family tree who have loved You and passed down a godly heritage to me. I praise You for being the same for all time!

EVENING

GOD'S PLANS

But the plans of the LORD stand firm forever, the purposes of his heart through all generations.

PSALM 33:11 NIV

Lord, Your plans for my life—for the whole world—are permanent. Nothing can interfere with or wreck Your plans. Whenever I feel like things are falling apart, remind me that they're not. With one glance, You see everything that has happened and hasn't happened yet. And You go ahead of me and prepare the way for me. Thank You, Lord! Amen.

MORNING

RICH IN GRACE

In him we have redemption through his blood, the forgiveness of sins, in accordance with the riches of God's grace.

EPHESIANS 1:7 NIV

Lord, the world tells me I should be rich by owning a lot of stuff, but You've taught me that I'm truly rich because of Your grace. Thank You that Your grace is great enough to cover my sins—every one of them. That's the kind of rich inheritance that I long for—and that You freely give!

EVENING

FOR GOOD HEALTH

"Say to him: 'Long life to you! Good health to you and your household! And good health to all that is yours!'"

1 SAMUEL 25:6 NIV

Lord, thank You for my good health. Help me take care of my body by eating healthy food, drinking enough water, and exercising. Give me the self-control I need to make wise choices. Help me see my body as You do: beautiful and wonderful and loved. Please keep me safe, Lord. Amen.

MORNING

RIGHTEOUS RULERS

"The one who rules righteously, who rules in the fear of God, is like the light of morning at sunrise, like a morning without clouds, like the gleaming of the sun on new grass after rain."

2 SAMUEL 23:3–4 NLT

Father God, this picture of rulers is so different from what I see today. I wouldn't describe any leaders in the beautiful way this verse does. Remind me to pray for people in authority, Lord. They need Your help to rule righteously.

EVENING

BREAKING FREE OF STRESS

Cast all your anxiety on him because he cares for you.

1 PETER 5:7 NIV

Lord, I didn't think much about stress when I was younger, but now with all my homework and after-school stuff, I get stressed out sometimes. Teach me how to balance everything I have to do. Teach me how to give You my stresses so I don't carry them around anymore. Thank You for caring about me, Lord, and for helping me when I'm stressed.

DAY 130

MORNING

A NEW COVENANT

"This is my blood of the covenant, which is poured out for many for the forgiveness of sins."
MATTHEW 26:28 NIV

Jesus, I've read in the Old Testament about the animal sacrifices people made so they could be forgiven. I'm glad I will never have to do that. Your blood that was shed when You died on the cross made up for everything everybody has done wrong. Thank You for the new promise—that I'm forgiven because of You.

EVENING

WHEN GOD DOESN'T HEAL

I am sure that our suffering now cannot be compared to the shining-greatness that He is going to give us.
ROMANS 8:18 NLV

Lord God, You have the power to heal anybody, so I struggle to understand why You don't always heal people when they're sick. Help me trust that any suffering we go through here on earth will be completely overshadowed by the great things You're going to do for us in heaven. Help me trust You.

DAY 131

MORNING

SPIRITUAL FITNESS

"Physical training is good, but training for godliness is much better, promising benefits in this life and in the life to come."

1 TIMOTHY 4:8 NLT

Father God, some people love to work out. I'm kind of in the middle: I don't hate exercising, but I don't love it either. And that's okay. You want me to take care of myself, but it shouldn't be an obsession. Spending time working on my soul is what makes me fit for this life—and for heaven!

EVENING

UNDER CONTROL

"The LORD is slow to anger, abounding in love and forgiving sin and rebellion. Yet he does not leave the guilty unpunished."

NUMBERS 14:18 NIV

Lord, sometimes I get so mad at people I want to scream! And I'm not alone. I see plenty of people who rant and rave when they're upset—especially on social media. But that's so unlike You. You want me to keep my emotions under control. You won't ignore my outbursts. Please help me imitate You.

MORNING

FAITHFUL TO FORGIVE

If we confess our sins, he is faithful and just to forgive us our sins, and to cleanse us from all unrighteousness.

1 JOHN 1:9 KJV

Father God, I confess that I've sinned. I've disobeyed You. Again and again, I go my own way. But every time, I have Your promise that You'll forgive me if I confess what I've done wrong and honestly want to change my behavior. Thank You for this promise, Lord.

EVENING

HOW BLESSED!

How blessed the people who have all this!
How blessed the people who have GOD for God!

PSALM 144:15 MSG

Just knowing You, Lord, is my greatest blessing. Nothing I could buy could fill me up like Your Spirit does. I'm always in the right place when I'm with You. I never lack anything because You give me everything. I want to remember Your blessings every second of my life. Thank You for *You*, Lord God. Thank You for being my God.

DAY 133

MORNING

COMFORTED

"Blessed are those who mourn,
for they shall be comforted."
MATTHEW 5:4 NKJV

Sorrow and happiness don't seem to go together, Lord. But I know that if I was never sad, I'd never know what Your comfort is like. Even on my most painful, tear-soaked days, You're able to make me feel all right inside. Thank You for comforting me. And when opportunities come my way to share Your comfort with others, please point them out. Amen.

EVENING

HELD TIGHT

"The God Who lives forever is your safe
place. His arms are always under you."
DEUTERONOMY 33:27 NLV

Lord, the wind is howling like some hideous beast tonight. The windows are even rattling! That's how I feel sometimes. I wonder how long I can hold on when bad things howl around me and shake me up inside. But I'm not really the one holding on, am I? You are there, holding me up, holding me tight. I'm safe with You—forever!

MORNING

POWER TO FORGIVE

"The Son of Man has power on earth to forgive sins."
MARK 2:10 NKJV

Jesus, no one else has the power to forgive sins like You do. You took the shame of my sins on Your shoulders as You hung on the cross. I'll never fully understand the pain You went through on that cross. But I'm eternally thankful for Your sacrifice. Thank You for Your power that sets me free from my sins. Amen.

EVENING

STRENGTH IN GOD

"Then you will have success if you are careful to observe the decrees and laws that the LORD gave Moses for Israel. Be strong and courageous. Do not be afraid or discouraged."
1 CHRONICLES 22:13 NIV

Lord, with You by my side, I can fend off fear. When I believe that You hold my future and guide me, strength and courage are mine. Help me cling to Your Word, Lord. I want to be where You can bless me.

DAY 135

MORNING

SLICE OF LIFE

Make the most of every opportunity in these evil days.
EPHESIANS 5:16 NLT

Lord, if I stare at a clock, the minutes seem to drag by, especially when I'm waiting for something to happen. I want time to go quicker. Help me remember that each minute is important. You've given me more than a thousand each day to make the most of. One minute is just a small slice of my life, but I don't want to waste it.

EVENING

REAL PROSPERITY

"Hear me, O Judah and you inhabitants of Jerusalem: Believe in the LORD your God, and you shall be established; believe His prophets, and you shall prosper."
2 CHRONICLES 20:20 NKJV

Father God, thank You for all the good things You've given me. Even when I'm going through hard times, don't let me become ungrateful. Remind me of all the ways I'm blessed. Without You, I could never have true peace or experience Your deep love. Thank You, Jesus, for all Your blessings.

MORNING

GOD'S NAME

Help us, God our Savior, for the glory of your name; deliver us and forgive our sins for your name's sake.

PSALM 79:9 NIV

I know my sins make me dirty, Lord. More than that, my sins separate me from You. But because You are who You are, You make me clean. You've got me covered. You deliver me from all my sins so that I can draw close to You, all to the glory of Your name! Thank You, Father!

EVENING

WE'LL MEET AGAIN

"I give them eternal life, and they shall never perish; no one will snatch them out of my hand."

JOHN 10:28 NIV

Father, I know that people who believe in You and who have made You Lord of their lives cannot die forever. Their earthly bodies may die, but their souls live on with You. You hold each of us safely in Your hand. Help me remember that even if someone I love dies—if they have received You—then we'll see each other again in heaven.

DAY 137

MORNING

A NEED MET

"First of all, look for the holy nation of God. Be right with Him. All these other things will be given to you also."
MATTHEW 6:33 NLV

Father God, I need new soccer cleats, but Mom says money is tight right now and I'll have to wait. Help me trust You. Help me focus on my relationship with You and not worry about whether I'll be able to play. Thank You for promising to meet my needs, even the little ones.

EVENING

A LITTLE FAITH

"If you had faith even as small as a mustard seed, you could say to this mulberry tree, 'May you be uprooted and be planted in the sea,' and it would obey you!"
LUKE 17:6 NLT

Thank You, Jesus, for the amazing things that happen when I have faith. It takes just a little to start big things. But when even a little faith seems hard to muster, remind me that all I have to do is ask for help and You'll be with me.

MORNING

FULLY FORGIVEN

Though we are overwhelmed by our sins, you forgive them all.

PSALM 65:3 NLT

I mess up a lot, Lord. In fact, sin seems stronger than me sometimes . . .especially this one sin (You know the one). It always seems to get me, and I feel powerless to change. Please wipe it out, Father God. I'll focus on You and Your Word, and I know You'll help me deal with this temptation. Thank You for forgiving me when I fail.

EVENING

GOD'S FAMILY NAME

"Whoever does God's will is
my brother and sister and mother."

MARK 3:35 NIV

Lord, just as I don't want to do things that will hurt my family's name, I don't want to do anything that will hurt Your name either. No one should blame You for my wrong actions. When I struggle to do what's right, remind me that I have a big Brother who helps me out in everything. Thank You for Jesus, Father God! Amen.

DAY 139

MORNING

BACKSLIDING

O LORD, though our iniquities testify against us, do it for Your name's sake; for our backslidings are many, we have sinned against You. . . . Yet You, O LORD, are in our midst. . .do not leave us!

JEREMIAH 14:7, 9 NKJV

No matter how far I go walking with You, Lord, I always start to slide backward. Some temptations keep tripping me up, and sometimes I sin. But You're still here with me. Don't leave me now.

EVENING

HEAVENLY FATHER

"No, the Father himself loves you because you have loved me and have believed that I came from God."

JOHN 16:27 NIV

Lord, You are my heavenly Father who never lets me down. Even when my mom or my dad disappoints me, I'm not alone. You love me and guide me. I'm so glad I'm part of Your family! I'll never be able to love You as much as You love me, but I can try!

DAY 140

MORNING

GARDENING

"For the Son of Man came to seek and to save the lost."

LUKE 19:10 NIV

Lord, You're a God who's not afraid of messes. You're not afraid to reach into the tangles and the muck. You see into the future of a lost person's heart: You see a garden where I see only a wilderness. I want to be like You. I want to love the lost like You do. Help me look past the mess to the soul inside. Amen.

EVENING

NO FEAR

The LORD is for me, so I will have no fear. What can mere people do to me? Yes, the LORD is for me; he will help me.

PSALM 118:6–7 NLT

What do I have to fear when You're on my side, Lord? Help me keep my eyes on You, even when life gets in the way. Turn my heart to Your truths, no matter what this world throws at me. I love and trust You, Lord.

DAY 141

MORNING

GETTING STARTED

The way of the sluggard is blocked with thorns.
PROVERBS 15:19 NIV

Father God, for me the first step toward a goal has always been the hardest, and I don't feel motivated to take this one now. I feel lazy. I know. I'm a procrastinator. I don't like to admit it, but You see it anyway. Thank You for giving me more chances than I deserve. Remind me that I just need to start. . .and You'll help me keep going.

EVENING

BLESSED WITH PEACE

The LORD will give strength to His people;
the LORD will bless His people with peace.
PSALM 29:11 NKJV

Your peace is my strength, Lord. When Your serenity fills my heart, I easily head Your way. I know where I need to go. Together we walk in the way that lasts forever. Thank You for promising me Your peace, and thank You that Your blessing is bigger than any problem I face! Pour out Your peace on my life so I can pass Your strength on to others.

MORNING

REBELLION

To the Lord our God belong mercies and forgivenesses, though we have rebelled against him.

DANIEL 9:9 KJV

Father God, sometimes I act like a child—I want to do what I want to do when I want to do it. I ignore what I know is right and do what isn't. I know I'm doing wrong. I rebel against Your love. Thank You for the forgiveness You so freely offer me when I turn to You in repentance, even though I don't deserve it. May I never take advantage of Your mercy.

EVENING

SEEK CHRIST NOW

Seek the LORD while He may be found, call upon Him while He is near.

ISAIAH 55:6 NKJV

You really want to save the lost and dying, Lord Jesus! You're so eager to wipe away our sins. It doesn't matter how old someone is when they cry out to You—You love to hear their voice. Lord, I pray that many, many, many more people would seek You while You may be found. And that's right now!

DAY 143

MORNING

TEACHER WOES

Whatever you do, work at it with all your heart, as working for the Lord, not for human masters.

COLOSSIANS 3:23 NIV

Dear Jesus, I have the most demanding teacher ever. I know I need to show her Your love, but I'm struggling! Please give me courage. Help me pray for my teacher and do my work as if it's an assignment from You. You, Lord, are the one I want to please most.

EVENING

MIRROR REFLECTION

We all, with open face beholding as in a glass the glory of the Lord, are changed into the same image from glory to glory, even as by the Spirit of the Lord.

2 CORINTHIANS 3:18 KJV

The more time I spend with You, Lord, the more I become like You. You began changing me the exact moment I received You as my Savior—actually, even before then! I can't wait for the day when I'm completely transformed, because I will see You!

MORNING

MERCIFUL

I will be merciful to their unrighteousness, and their sins and their iniquities will I remember no more.

HEBREWS 8:12 KJV

Lord, thank You that You are a merciful God. You don't even remember all the times I let You down! You truly forgive and forget. Teach me how to show that kind of mercy to the people in my life who have wronged me. I want to shine Your light on them by reflecting Your unconditional love.

EVENING

WORK IT OUT

Dear friends, you always followed my instructions when I was with you. And now that I am away, it is even more important. Work hard to show the results of your salvation, obeying God with deep reverence and fear.

PHILIPPIANS 2:12 NLT

God, because You have saved me and made me Your child, I know I'll spend eternity with You. But how I live my life today still matters. Help me show that I'm saved. Help me obey You and honor You in everything.

DAY 145

MORNING

DIFFICULT PEOPLE

Bear with each other and forgive one another if any of you has a grievance against someone.

COLOSSIANS 3:13 NIV

Dear Lord, I ask You to help me be patient and kind today. That's what I need as I deal with difficult people and irritating situations. In those moments when I want to scream, help me remember to forgive. It's just so easy to react, but help me choose my response instead. I'm depending on Your power, Lord. Amen.

EVENING

HIS PERFECT WAY

As for God, his way is perfect; the word of the LORD is tried: he is a buckler to all them that trust in him.

2 SAMUEL 22:31 KJV

Your way is perfect, Lord. You will never steer me wrong. When I'm confused, wondering what my next step should be, Your Word guides me. It answers my questions about life, tells me how to handle relationships, and encourages me. You've given me all I need to succeed.

MORNING

DELIGHTED IN MERCY

Who is a God like You, Who forgives sin and the wrong-doing of Your chosen people who are left? He does not stay angry forever because He is happy to show loving-kindness.

MICAH 7:18 NLV

God, sometimes when I ask for Your forgiveness for a repeat sin, I assume that while You do forgive me, You're doing it begrudgingly. But the truth is You're happy to show loving-kindness! You don't stay angry. I'm so relieved and so thankful!

EVENING

MEDITATE ON THE WORD

"Study this Book of Instruction continually. Meditate on it day and night so you will be sure to obey everything written in it. Only then will you prosper and succeed in all you do."

JOSHUA 1:8 NLT

I'm distracted by a lot of things, Lord. Sometimes it's hard to stop for one minute and focus on reading the Bible. But I know how important it is. Help me read attentively and really think over what I've read. Amen.

DAY 147

MORNING

BIRDSONG

"The LORD your God in your midst, the Mighty One, will save; He will rejoice over you with gladness, He will quiet you with His love, He will rejoice over you with singing."

ZEPHANIAH 3:17 NKJV

Father God, the birds singing outside today make me so happy. They're like sequins in the world! Help me remember that as much as I love listening to birds, You rejoice over me even more. Thank You for Your love, Lord—and for the birds too!

EVENING

DAILY GROWTH

Like newborn babies, you must crave pure spiritual milk so that you will grow into a full experience of salvation.

1 PETER 2:2 NLT

Lord, lambs are so cute! I've seen them run and play and then trot back to their mom to nurse. They know what to do without even thinking about it. Help me crave Your Word just like those lambs crave milk. Let Your words nourish me so I'll keep growing in my faith every day.

MORNING

BLOTTED OUT

"I, even I, am He who blots out your transgressions for My own sake; and I will not remember your sins."
ISAIAH 43:25 NKJV

Father God, I'm so thankful You don't hold grudges. I praise You because not only have You wiped away my sins, You don't even remember them! You wipe my slate clean; You give me a new start; You hit the RESET button. You've made me really, truly free from all I've done wrong.

EVENING

I WILL REJOICE

"Now is your time of grief, but I will see you again and you will rejoice, and no one will take away your joy."
JOHN 16:22 NIV

You're with me, Jesus. What more could I want? Just being with You makes me sing inside, even when I'm going through tough situations. That's a joy no one can steal from me! Let my life overflow with Your joy so much that everyone who sees it will want to know You.

DAY 149

MORNING

FAR, FAR AWAY

He has taken our sins from us as far as the east is from the west.

PSALM 103:12 NLV

Father God, whenever I feel like I'm a hopeless case—like I'll never be able to get rid of sin in my life—remind me that, from Your perspective, my soul and my sin might as well be in different dimensions. You take my sins far, far away from me. Help me trust that I'm *completely* forgiven. Amen.

EVENING

PERFECT PEACE

You will keep in perfect peace those whose minds are steadfast, because they trust in you.

ISAIAH 26:3 NIV

Lord, this verse is a promise and a challenge. You promise to keep me in perfect peace—without any worries at all—but I have to keep my mind on You. If my mind is bouncing from one worry to another, there's no way I'll be at peace. But when I focus on You—trusting You with my whole self—You'll give me Your perfect peace and rest!

MORNING

GOOGOLPLEX

He counts the number of the stars; He calls them all by name. Great is our Lord, and mighty in power; His understanding is infinite.

PSALM 147:4–5 NKJV

God, You are infinite. As much as I want to think about You in this way, my mind keeps trying to make You smaller—something I can wrap my brain around. So today I'll just praise You for how infinitely great You are. I'm happy to be a speck in Your loving hand.

EVENING

UNTROUBLED

"Peace I leave with you; my peace I give you. I do not give to you as the world gives. Do not let your hearts be troubled and do not be afraid."

JOHN 14:27 NIV

Following You is nothing like living as part of the world, Lord. People living apart from You worry about the future. Their search for rest never ends. But You give a kind of peace that gets me through even the most difficult situations. Please turn my heart to trust in You so I'm always untroubled.

DAY 151

MORNING

BEHIND GOD'S BACK

Surely it was for my benefit that I suffered such anguish.
In your love you kept me from the pit of destruction;
you have put all my sins behind your back.

ISAIAH 38:17 NIV

Father God, when You put something behind Your back, it doesn't exist anymore. You don't want to look at it or think about it. You're not even bothered by it. Remind me that this is what You've done with my sins. They're gone!

EVENING

JOY IN SORROW

Light shines on the righteous and joy on the upright in heart. Rejoice in the LORD, you who are righteous, and praise his holy name.

PSALM 97:11–12 NIV

I may not feel joyful right now, Lord, but I trust You to keep Your promises. Just because today doesn't seem wonderful doesn't mean You've forgotten me. Your light still guides me. Thank You for Your faithfulness. Thank You for being there, willing to help me no matter what.

MORNING

SATISFIED

The poor will eat and be satisfied; those who seek the LORD will praise him—may your hearts live forever!
PSALM 22:26 NIV

I know I'm saved by You, Lord, but sometimes my heart still feels empty. If my heart echoes with doubt, it's only because I'm not trusting You all the way. I want to be content right here, right now, with the blessings You've given me. Help me seek You and be satisfied. I praise You, Lord! Amen.

EVENING

GRACE IN THE NOT-KNOWING

So when. . .this mortal has put on immortality, then shall be brought to pass the saying that is written: "Death is swallowed up in victory."
1 CORINTHIANS 15:54 NKJV

Lord, tonight I've cried and cried, and You've listened and loved me and comforted me with words from the Bible. Someone I love is gone. I don't understand why she had to die, but I'm going to trust You to help me through this and give me hope.

DAY 153

MORNING

UNLIMITED RESOURCES

"For every animal of the forest is mine, and the cattle on a thousand hills."

PSALM 50:10 NIV

Heavenly Father, You have unlimited resources. Everything belongs to You. So I'm asking You to supply a special need for my family today. I know You can fix this situation, if fixing it is what's good for us. Because You're my Father, I'm asking for Your help. We need You to provide. We need You with us to get through this difficult time.

EVENING

TAUGHT BY GOD

"All your children shall be taught by the LORD, and great shall be the peace of your children."

ISAIAH 54:13 NKJV

No teacher could be greater than You, Lord. When we learn from You, we discover all we need to know about the world. We have no reason to fear, for we've been instructed by the Master Himself. Someday, if I have kids of my own, I want to dedicate myself to helping them discover the lessons You're teaching me.

MORNING

THE DEPTHS OF THE SEA

You will again have compassion on us;
you will tread our sins underfoot and hurl all
our iniquities into the depths of the sea.
MICAH 7:19 NIV

Thank You for Your loving compassion, Father, that throws my sin to the bottom of the deepest ocean, never to be thought of again. Take all the selfish urges of my heart and trample them; subdue them, so that I'm free to serve You with nothing holding me back.

EVENING

STRENGTH AND PEACE

The LORD gives strength to his people;
the LORD blesses his people with peace.
PSALM 29:11 NIV

Lord, it's interesting the way You couple strength and peace. They don't necessarily seem to go together. Still, I'm thinking of a father as he plays with his kids. He's strong and could easily hurt them, but he loves them and keeps his strength under control. They feel safe and loved. . .and at peace. That's how we, Your children, feel with You, Lord. Amen.

MORNING

NEW CLOTHES

The angel said. . . , "Take off his dirty clothes." And he said to him, "See, I have taken your sin away from you, and will dress you in beautiful clothes."
ZECHARIAH 3:4 NLV

Lord, You offer me a brand-new wardrobe to replace my filthy clothes that are stained with sin. Forgive me when I think my dirty rags are enough and I try to hold on to them. Help me put on the new clothes You give me.

EVENING

CREATED FOR A PURPOSE

For by Him all things were created that are in heaven and that are on earth, visible and invisible, whether thrones or dominions or principalities or powers. All things were created through Him and for Him.
COLOSSIANS 1:16 NKJV

Father God, when You spoke this world into existence and when You formed me with Your hands, those weren't just random acts of Your power. All creation, including me, is intended to glorify and praise You. Help me do just that.

MORNING

THE WEB

I will set no sinful thing in front of my eyes.
PSALM 101:3 NLV

Lord, I can't really imagine my life without the internet, but I know it's not all good. I can get caught going to sites I shouldn't, like a bug caught in a spider's web. I can get stuck in negativity and gossip and even low self-esteem when I get sucked into social media. Please, Lord, help me be smart about the internet. Amen.

EVENING

SHINING LIGHTS

You are God's children and no one can talk against you, even in a sin-loving and sin-sick world. You are to shine as lights among the sinful people of this world.
PHILIPPIANS 2:15 NLV

Lord, I love being outside in the sunshine. And at night I'm glad to turn on the lights. Light brightens. And that's what I want to do. I want my friends and neighbors—everyone!—to see You in me. Let me be a light for You.

MORNING

SHOWERED

"Then I will put clean water on you, and you will be clean. I will make you clean from all your unclean ways and from all your false gods."

EZEKIEL 36:25 NLV

Each time I take a shower, Lord, remind me that You've showered my soul with Your love. As I lather up with soap, remind me of the cleansing power of Your grace and mercy. You wash away everything in me that is false, making me truly clean.

EVENING

THE JOY OF THE LORD IS MY STRENGTH

For the joy of the LORD is your strength.

NEHEMIAH 8:10 KJV

I'm tired today, Lord. There were moments when I thought I couldn't take another step. The truth is I can't move forward without You. But You are with me. You want to take the pressure off me. I have Your joy when I walk with You and draw strength from You. Just to be with You, Lord, is an amazing gift.

MORNING

GREAT LOVE

For great is his love toward us, and the faithfulness of the LORD endures forever. Praise the LORD.

PSALM 117:2 NIV

I have so much to praise You for, Lord. One bad thing happening can't close the door on all You've done for me and all You're going to do for me. Each time I pray, Your Holy Spirit fills me with comfort. I praise You for the love and faithfulness You've poured out in my life. Thank You, Jesus.

EVENING

A GOOD LAND

"For the LORD your God is bringing you into a good land, a land of brooks of water, of fountains and springs, that flow out of valleys and hills."

DEUTERONOMY 8:7 NKJV

Lord, thank You for the way rain droplets spangle tree branches like diamonds. Thank You for the pictures You paint each sunset. Thank You for spring flowers at the end of winter. Thank You for the beauty of Your Word and Your world. Amen.

DAY 159

MORNING

WHENEVER I PRAY

"And when you stand praying, if you hold anything against anyone, forgive them, so that your Father in heaven may forgive you your sins."

MARK 11:25 NIV

Whenever I pray to You, Lord, asking You to do something for me, remind me first to let go of any unforgiveness I have in my heart. I don't want to be a grudge holder. Harboring resentment hurts me more than it hurts the other person anyway. Help me forgive like You do.

EVENING

IN THE RIGHT DIRECTION

He guides the humble in what is right and teaches them his way.

PSALM 25:9 NIV

Lord, when I sit at Your feet and am willing to listen to You, You set me on the glory road. I can't imagine living without Your guidance. So many blessings come from living for You that I wouldn't want to live any other way. Please show me all I need to know today, Lord. Lead me in the right direction. Amen.

DAY 160

MORNING

ACTIONS SHOW OUR FAITH

Faith by itself isn't enough. Unless it produces good deeds, it is dead and useless.

JAMES 2:17 NLT

Lord, I know that genuine faith will show up in good deeds. So I pray for wisdom to know what You've called me to do. Help me know the right thing to do and the best time to do it. Grow authentic faith in me, Lord. I want to do every single good thing You've planned for me.

EVENING

EVEN THOUGH

"Even though He would kill me, yet I will trust in Him."

JOB 13:15 NLV

Dear Lord, tonight as the sun set, the horror of this world seemed to hit me. Yes, there are butterflies and rainbows and smiles, but there are also broken things and troubles and frowns. It's hard to know what to do with all this beauty so mixed up with ugliness. I'm crying out to You. Help me trust Your love as I try to understand.

MORNING

SHINING BRIGHT

"In the same way, let your light shine before others, that they may see your good deeds and glorify your Father in heaven."
MATTHEW 5:16 NIV

Dear God, I want to show off who You are. Every day I interact with people who aren't believers. I want my light to shine for them. Let me sense Your nudges today. Let my life speak to people about how You change us and how good You are. In Jesus' name. Amen.

EVENING

POINTING TO GOD

When you are around people who do not know God, be careful how you act. Even if they talk against you as wrong-doers, in the end they will give thanks to God for your good works when Christ comes again.
1 PETER 2:12 NLV

Father, some people might look for evidence in my life to discredit what I say I believe. Help me live in such a way that they won't find anything. My purpose is to draw others to You.

MORNING

OVERLOOKING OFFENSES

A person's wisdom yields patience;
it is to one's glory to overlook an offense.
PROVERBS 19:11 NIV

The word *glory* has to do with light. Lord, remind me that I'm most truly myself—my best and shiniest self—when I don't act on my anger against others. Give me wisdom to know how to respond to people and situations in the same way You would. Let love, respect, and kindness be at the root of everything I do.

EVENING

GREAT RICHES

One person pretends to be rich, yet has nothing;
another pretends to be poor, yet has great wealth.
PROVERBS 13:7 NIV

Lord, sometimes I begin thinking about how much better life would be if I had loads of money. I could buy anything, so I'd never feel like I was missing out. But I have to say thank You for this verse. It reminds me that money isn't everything and that I'm better off—*richer*—when my life is focused on You.

DAY 163

MORNING

HOLES

He also brought me up out of a horrible pit. . . .
He has put a new song in my mouth—praise to our God.
PSALM 40:2–3 NKJV

Lord, when You found me stuck in a hole I made myself, all I wanted to do was pull the dirt down over my head. But You didn't let me. And You didn't just reach out to me; You jumped *in*. Thank You for changing the ending of my story, Lord.

EVENING

SOWING AND REAPING

Remember this—a farmer who plants only a
few seeds will get a small crop. But the one who
plants generously will get a generous crop.
2 CORINTHIANS 9:6 NLT

It makes sense, Lord. . .if I don't plant a lot, I'll never get a lot back. I know "planting" here doesn't refer to actual seeds. It means the effort and time and talents that I put into cultivating my spiritual life and helping others. May I plant generously!

MORNING

PERSECUTION

"But I tell you, love those who hate you. . . . Pray for those who do bad things to you and who make it hard for you."
MATTHEW 5:44 NLV

Father God, I struggle with the idea of loving people who hurt me just because I believe in You. Even now believers are being persecuted all over the world, and the suffering they experience is so unfair. But help me obey Your command to love haters. Help me pray for them. Who knows? Maybe You'll turn their lives around!

EVENING

SPIRITUAL COURAGE

"Be strong and very courageous. Be careful to obey all the law my servant Moses gave you; do not turn from it to the right or to the left, that you may be successful wherever you go."
JOSHUA 1:7 NIV

I can't go wrong, Lord, when I'm obeying You. It's only when I turn from Your ways that I get into trouble. Help me stay on track with You. Thank You for giving me courage, because I couldn't do it without You.

DAY 165

MORNING

BLESSINGS INSTEAD OF CURSES

"Bless those who curse you,
pray for those who mistreat you."
LUKE 6:28 NIV

Lord, I feel misused. I feel offended and abused. I'm angry and hurt. I come to You with these feelings and give them all to You. Please take away the hurt and my desire for revenge. Give me Your heart when it comes to those who have mistreated me. I pray You would bless the people who have made me feel this way.

EVENING

BE CONTENT

Keep your lives free from the love of money.
Be happy with what you have. God has said,
"I will never leave you or let you be alone."
HEBREWS 13:5 NLV

Lord, I'm often tempted to complain. I see the gifts that others have received from You and wonder why You haven't given them to me. But then I remember that *You're* a gift, and You've given me much more than I deserve. Help me be content.

MORNING

A HOLY FIRE

For our God is a consuming fire.
HEBREWS 12:29 NKJV

Father God, when I'm cold, all I want to do is cuddle up in a fleecy robe and drink hot chocolate. Thank You for never letting me be really, truly cold. You've always provided a warm place for me to live. Your love never grows cold either. You're a constant source of light and warmth for my soul. And You are with me through each fiery trial.

EVENING

THE SPIRIT IN ME

The Spirit of God, who raised Jesus from the dead, lives in you.
ROMANS 8:11 NLT

Lord Jesus, the same powerful Spirit who brought You back to life after You'd been dead for three days is the same Spirit who now lives in me. What a mind-blowing truth! I'll never know everything this means for me, but I know He makes me alive and able to live for You. Thank You for the Holy Spirit, Jesus. Thank You!

DAY 167

MORNING

FACING THE TRUTH

The human spirit is the lamp of the LORD
that sheds light on one's inmost being.
PROVERBS 20:27 NIV

Lord, thank You for accepting me as I am, where I am, today. You see the potential of who I can be, even when I can't see it. Show me the things in my heart that You want to change. Open my eyes—I don't want to pretend anymore. Help me see the truth so You can make me new!

EVENING

I BLEW IT

If we confess our sins, He is faithful and just to forgive
us our sins and to cleanse us from all unrighteousness.
1 JOHN 1:9 NKJV

Lord, I blew it today. I wish I could take back my attitude and words. Sometimes I don't understand how You can still love me, but You do. Please forgive me. Please clean up my messiness. And next time, help me do the things that You'd approve of.

MORNING

INHERITING A BLESSING

Do not repay evil with evil or insult with insult. On the contrary, repay evil with blessing, because to this you were called so that you may inherit a blessing.

1 PETER 3:9 NIV

When I'm hurt, Lord, my first reaction is to strike back. Turn that tendency inside out, I pray, so my first reaction is to bless. When I feel like I can't, remind me that You'll give me countless blessings in return.

EVENING

CONFIDENCE IN HIM

My old self has been crucified with Christ. It is no longer I who live, but Christ lives in me. So I live in this earthly body by trusting in the Son of God, who loved me and gave himself for me.

GALATIANS 2:20 NLT

When people see me, Lord, let them see You. Help me not to confuse who You say I am with arrogance or pride. My confidence is only because You live in and through me.

MORNING

PUT UP WITH IT!

We speak kind words to those who speak against us. When people hurt us, we say nothing.

1 CORINTHIANS 4:12 NLV

Lord, You know the things that push my buttons—the things that get under my skin. Give me the patience to put up with them. I know You'll use every situation to bring about Your will, but some situations are especially tough! Please give me the composure and encouragement I need to endure.

EVENING

A POSITIVE PERSPECTIVE

You are a chosen people, a royal priesthood, a holy nation, God's special possession, that you may declare the praises of him who called you out of darkness into his wonderful light.

1 PETER 2:9 NIV

Father God, as I learn who I am in Christ, I realize I need to look at life positively. My life in You isn't about what I'm missing or don't have. It's about Your wonderful light that illuminates my way so I never need to walk in darkness. I have everything I need in You!

MORNING

L-O-V-E

"For God so loved the world that He gave His only begotten Son, that whoever believes in Him should not perish but have everlasting life."

JOHN 3:16 NKJV

Father God, *love* is such a little word, just four letters. Most of the time, I don't think about the power of that word: how it can move mountains, calm storms, heal the sick, redeem sinners. That word saved me from hell. I love You, Lord. Let me never stop counting the ways.

EVENING

THE BEST ROUTE

I will instruct you and teach you in the way you should go; I will guide you with My eye.

PSALM 32:8 NKJV

Lord, thank You for setting me on a new course and guiding me through each moment of confusion or trouble. I'm so glad You don't expect me to figure out some difficult road map. When it comes to doing Your will, Your Word offers clear direction. Let every path I take be one that pleases You.

MORNING

KEEP ME

Keep me as the apple of your eye;
hide me in the shadow of your wings.
PSALM 17:8 NIV

Father God, I often forget to be thankful for important things. So many times You've protected me, and I didn't know it until later. Although I'm the apple of Your eye, I realize I'm not immune to trauma and disaster. I'm grateful that You care about me and that nothing can touch me unless it has passed Your inspection.

EVENING

NEW LIFE IN CHRIST

Anyone who belongs to Christ has become a new person. The old life is gone; a new life has begun!
2 CORINTHIANS 5:17 NLT

Heavenly Father, in Your love and mercy, You saved me. I was lost and alone, but You found me. You picked me up and gave me a new life. All I had to do was believe and receive this gift. Thank You for Your incredible kindness! Continue to make me new each day in Christ.

MORNING

FEEDING MY ENEMIES

*"If your enemy is hungry, feed him;
if he is thirsty, give him a drink."*
ROMANS 12:20 NKJV

It's not enough to *forgive* my enemies, Lord—You also ask me to be good to them by actively meeting their needs. I'm hurting so much right now that I can't do this on my own. Please show me what to do and give me the strength to do it. May I look for opportunities to help those who have hurt me.

EVENING

LET LOVE RULE

"Live out your God-created identity. Live generously and graciously toward others, the way God lives toward you."
MATTHEW 5:48 MSG

Heavenly Father, help me get rid of anger and insults. I have the mind of Christ and can exercise self-control. Show me how to live my life with mercy, kindness, humility, gentleness, and patience. Remind me to be quick to forgive. Above all, help me let Christ govern my heart. Please forgive me when I forget.

DAY 173

MORNING

WAITING FOR GOD

Do not say, "I'll pay you back for this wrong!"
Wait for the LORD, and he will avenge you.
PROVERBS 20:22 NIV

Father God, when a wrong has been done, I feel like I should do something about it *right now*. Teach me to wait for You instead. You're in charge of righting wrongs. Give me Your wisdom in every situation; and when the time is right, show me what to say and do in order to glorify You.

EVENING

COMPASSION

Be kind and compassionate to one another, forgiving
each other, just as in Christ God forgave you.
EPHESIANS 4:32 NIV

Lord, Your compassion for people is huge. You're loving and kind to everyone—including me! Where would I be without Your compassion? Help me be like You, Lord. Create in me a heart like Yours. Open my eyes so I see when those around me need some compassion. Help me be patient and forgive people when they're not at their best.

MORNING

SIBLINGS

Whoever claims to love God yet hates a brother or sister is a liar. For whoever does not love their brother and sister, whom they have seen, cannot love God, whom they have not seen.

1 JOHN 4:20 NIV

Heavenly Father, thank You for my siblings. We may fight sometimes, but I know I can depend on them to be there for me. They understand me like no one else. Bless my brothers and sisters today. In Jesus' name. Amen.

EVENING

A TRUE FRIEND

"Is this the way you treat your friend David?" Absalom asked him. "Why aren't you with him?"

2 SAMUEL 16:17 NLT

Lord, I want to be a better friend. Help me be devoted, trustworthy, and reliable. Help me think of what my friends need instead of what I need all the time. When they're struggling, help me stick by them so they know they're not alone. Make me a true friend—a friend just like You've been to me.

MORNING

HE IS WILLING

Jesus reached out his hand and touched the man. "I am willing," he said. "Be clean!" Immediately he was cleansed of his leprosy.

MATTHEW 8:3 NIV

Lord, I'm amazed by Your love! For a holy God, sin is worse than leprosy. You can't even look at it. Yet through Jesus, You made a way to cleanse people from sin. I'm not a leper, but my life does get stained by sin. And again and again, You're willing to reach out and make me clean with Your love. Thank You!

EVENING

PERFECT COUNSELOR

"He will not speak on His own authority, but whatever He hears He will speak; and He will tell you things to come."

JOHN 16:13 NKJV

Lord, when I ask for advice from a lot of people but only end up more confused, maybe the problem is that I haven't turned to the perfect counselor—You. Even the most discerning person won't always know what to say. No one can guide me like You can. Thank You for giving me Your Spirit's direction.

MORNING

THE OTHER CHEEK

*"If anyone slaps you on the right cheek,
turn to them the other cheek also."*
MATTHEW 5:39 NIV

So. . .if someone hurts me, Lord, I'm supposed to let them hurt me again? That doesn't seem right. Isn't that asking too much? What about standing up for myself? Teach me what Jesus meant when He said this. Help me study His example in the Bible, and then give me a heart that wants to follow Him.

EVENING

PLEASING WORDS

*May the words of my mouth and the meditation of my heart
be pleasing to you, O LORD, my rock and my redeemer.*
PSALM 19:14 NLT

Lord, the Bible tells me that the tongue is powerful. Sometimes I say things I don't mean or that I regret saying. Fill my spirit with Your goodness as Your words of life bring health to my body. Help me control what I say by thinking about what pleases You before I open my mouth.

DAY 177

MORNING

FOLLOWING GOOD

See that no one renders evil for evil to anyone, but always pursue what is good both for yourselves and for all.

1 THESSALONIANS 5:15 NKJV

Even when I see evil all around me, Lord, help me to chase after what's good rather than what's bad. Forgive me when I'm lured by the fake shininess that evil often hides behind. Keep me from falling for the tricks of the devil, and keep my feet on Your path—the good and right path.

EVENING

COMPLETELY WHOLE

People with their minds set on you, you keep completely whole, steady on their feet, because they keep at it and don't quit.

ISAIAH 26:3 MSG

Lord, I give my worries to You in prayer, but later I take them back. Somewhere in my thinking, I stop trusting You and try to work out my problems on my own. Forgive me for not trusting You. Show me how to give my worries completely to You, because then You'll keep me completely whole.

MORNING

THE PROMISE KEEPER

For no matter how many promises God has made, they are "Yes" in Christ.

2 CORINTHIANS 1:20 NIV

Lord, I haven't always kept my promises. I promised to help a friend with a project, and then I forgot. I promised to play a game with my sister, and then I got too busy. I promised my mom I'd clean my room, and then I spent all day watching videos. . . Thank You that You *always* keep Your promises.

EVENING

TEACHABLE

Pay attention to what I say; turn your ear to my words. Do not let them out of your sight, keep them within your heart; for they are life to those who find them and health to one's whole body.

PROVERBS 4:20–22 NIV

Holy Spirit, please be my teacher. Show me how to let go of selfishness and stubbornness and listen to You. Help me focus on Your words and keep them in my heart. I want to go where You want me to go and do what You want me to do.

MORNING

PEOPLE'S PLANS AND GOD'S PURPOSE

You can make many plans,
but the LORD's purpose will prevail.
PROVERBS 19:21 NLT

Father God, You know the plans in my mind and the desires in my heart. But the Bible says it's Your purpose that will rule the day. Help me get out of the way if I'm blocking You. Help me stay confident in Your Word and Your plan for my life, even when I want something different. I'll be listening for Your instructions today.

EVENING

WHAT LOVE DOES

Love takes everything that comes without giving up. Love believes all things. Love hopes for all things. Love keeps on in all things.
1 CORINTHIANS 13:7 NLV

Give me a loving heart, Lord. Help me be a loving friend to others, always hoping and believing for the best. Remind me that love is an everyday action, not just something to show when I feel like it. Help me express love in words too. Thank You for being the perfect example of love.

MORNING

THE ETERNAL SECURITY SYSTEM

For he will order his angels to protect you wherever you go.
PSALM 91:11 NLT

Father God, Your Word says Your mighty angels protect us. They go with us and defend us when we're following Your way. There have been times in my life when I was very much aware of Your protection. Thank You, Lord, for the invisible guardians who surround me and keep me from harm. Amen.

EVENING

UNDESERVED PAIN

If you suffer for doing good and endure it patiently, God is pleased with you.
1 PETER 2:20 NLT

Lord, pain and the joys of Your kingdom don't seem to go together, yet You experienced both on the cross. I can't understand it all, but You promise that patiently putting up with undeserved pain isn't for nothing. And You are pleased with me when I endure each trial, big or small. Help me give You that joy today.

DAY 181

MORNING

SPIRITUAL GUARDRAILS

Stay alert! Watch out for your great enemy, the devil. He prowls around like a roaring lion, looking for someone to devour.

1 PETER 5:8 NLT

Dear Father God, help me put up boundaries in my life. I don't want to fall prey to sin because I wasn't being careful. Just like guardrails on a dangerous highway, boundaries in my life keep me closer to the center and farther away from the cliffs. Please help me to center my life on You.

EVENING

A GIRL WHO FEARS THE LORD

Charm is deceptive, and beauty does not last; but a woman who fears the LORD will be greatly praised.

PROVERBS 31:30 NLT

Lord, I want to be a Proverbs 31 girl. My focus shouldn't be on the way I look or the clothes and jewelry I wear. Other people should notice my heart that seeks You always and wants to respect and honor You in everything. My greatest desire is to be known as Your daughter.

MORNING

QUARRELS

Bear with each other and forgive one another
if any of you has a grievance against someone.
Forgive as the Lord forgave you.
COLOSSIANS 3:13 NIV

It doesn't take much to make people fight, does it, God? The smallest thing can annoy us, and then we're off and yelling. Remind me that You have forgiven me for huge offenses. Help me bite my tongue before I start an argument. Forgive me when I do quarrel, and help me forgive others too.

EVENING

KEEPING PROMISES TO MYSELF

Each of you must take responsibility for doing the
creative best you can with your own life.
GALATIANS 6:5 MSG

Lord, I make promises to myself and don't always keep them. Help me remember that I'm responsible to You for the way my life turns out. Give me the strength to stick to my goals. Remind me that it's okay to do good things for myself that help me become the person You created me to be.

DAY 183

MORNING

RULE OF LOVE

"To him who sits on the throne and to the Lamb be praise and honor and glory and power, for ever and ever!"

REVELATION 5:13 NIV

Father God, You are Lord of the universe, yet You left Your throne and came down to earth to be near us. You give and sustain life, yet You sacrificed Your Son to save us. What You did for us makes no earthly sense. But You did it, and I'm forever grateful!

EVENING

A FUTURE FOR ME

Consider the blameless, observe the upright; a future awaits those who seek peace.

PSALM 37:37 NIV

Lord, this verse describes me! I'm blameless because You've forgiven me. I'm upright because You made me right with You and hold me up as I follow Your ways. I'm a peace seeker because I want to be like You. Absolutely nothing can harm me when I'm living so close to You. My future is absolutely safe in Your hands. Amen!

MORNING

TENDERHEARTED

And be kind to one another, tenderhearted, forgiving one another, even as God in Christ forgave you.

EPHESIANS 4:32 NKJV

The world may think a tender heart is a weakness, but I know better, Lord. Your heart is tender toward me, and You're quick to show me grace. Give me a tender heart too. Guard my heart so it won't become callous to the hurts and evils affecting those around me. Fill me with Your kindness so I can love freely and forgive generously.

EVENING

STANDING FOR THE TRUTH

For we cannot oppose the truth, but must always stand for the truth.

2 CORINTHIANS 13:8 NLT

Father God, You've given me the values of honor and truth. I don't want to bend those values or make compromises. Other people might act without integrity, but I know I'll only hurt myself and You if I follow their example. Help me choose what is right and just—*always*. Thank You for reminding me of the way I need to go.

DAY 185

MORNING

MOTHER'S DAY ANY DAY

"As a mother comforts her child, so will I comfort you."

ISAIAH 66:13 NIV

Lord, I thank You for my mom. She loved me before I was born. She has loved me through every scraped knee and bad attitude. She loves me a lot like You love me, and I'm so glad to be loved like that! Bless her today, Lord, and show me how I can let her know how special her love is to me.

EVENING

SETTING AN EXAMPLE

In everything set them an example by doing what is good. In your teaching show integrity, seriousness and soundness of speech.

TITUS 2:7–8 NIV

Lord, I've never really thought of myself as a model Christian, but I can be an example to my friends. The Bible shows me what is good, and I can live it out for others to see. I can teach what I've been taught. Help me do what is good, Lord. Help me set a great example that others will follow.

MORNING

OVERCOMING

Do not be overcome by evil,
but overcome evil with good.
ROMANS 12:21 NKJV

When darkness seems to be attacking me from all sides, Lord, give me Your strength so I can rise above the world's evil. Make Your Spirit strong in me so I can feel You near me. Help me bring Your goodness into any situation. Use me in whatever way You can for Your will to be done. I'm an overcomer through You!

EVENING

WHOLE AND HEALTHY

Do not be wise in your own eyes; fear the LORD
and shun evil. This will bring health to your
body and nourishment to your bones.
PROVERBS 3:7–8 NIV

Lord, sometimes I think I know what's best for me. But You've proved over and over that You know best. It's when I respect You and follow Your ways that I'm whole and healthy in soul and body. Help me be wise in *Your* eyes by seeking Your wisdom.

DAY 187

MORNING

CONTENT NO MATTER WHAT

I am not saying this because I am in need, for I have learned to be content whatever the circumstances.
PHILIPPIANS 4:11 NIV

Lord, right now I'm feeling great, so it's easy to be content. Other times I've believed the lie that aches and pains and hard times mean You're not blessing me anymore. The truth? I'm complete in Christ no matter what's going on. I can be content whatever the circumstances! Thank You, Lord. Amen.

EVENING

HOPE IN CHRIST

All men will die as Adam died. But all those who belong to Christ will be raised to new life.
1 CORINTHIANS 15:22 NLV

Father God, I'm so glad that death doesn't have the last word. You sent Jesus to overthrow death and offer life to those who put their faith in Him. The "unchangeable" pattern of death died on the cross, and there is no greater hope than that! Help me hold on to You and Your promise, no matter what.

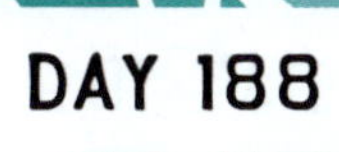

DAY 188

MORNING

PASSION AND PURPOSE

Because we are united with Christ, we have received an inheritance from God, for he chose us in advance, and he makes everything work out according to his plan.
EPHESIANS 1:11 NLT

Father, I'm feeling bored. I know there are parts of life that aren't particularly exciting. But living without passion and purpose isn't what You have in mind for us. Show me how to find meaning in my everyday life. Open up my eyes to see Your amazing plan.

EVENING

CONSTANT LOVE

A friend loves at all times.
PROVERBS 17:17 NKJV

All I need is love! But I'm wondering, Lord, if I've always loved my friends. I mean that constant, enduring, unyielding love—Your kind of love. Forgive me for those times when I was so caught up in myself and my day that I didn't show love to a friend who really needed it. Fill me and my friends with Your love, and help us share it with everyone around us.

MORNING

HOLY COPYCATS

Therefore be imitators of God as dear children.
EPHESIANS 5:1 NKJV

Brothers and sisters fight a lot. My siblings and I prove that! But remind me, Father, that we are Your kids and should be following You, not fighting with each other. Give us an abundance of grace when we're dealing with each other, and help us keep our eyes on You as we work things out. If we're copying You, Lord, we'll be blessed beyond imagination.

EVENING

GOD'S COMMITMENT

Remember his covenant forever—the commitment he made to a thousand generations.
1 CHRONICLES 16:15 NLT

Lord, I want the whole world to know what You've done for me. You've changed my life. I was lost, and You found me. You created me and crowned me with Your glory. You take responsibility for me, whether I succeed or fail. Everything I need is found in You. Every promise You've made, You keep. Generation after generation depends on You, just like I do.

MORNING

MERCIFUL LIKE GOD

"Therefore be merciful, just as your Father also is merciful."

LUKE 6:36 NKJV

Father, I'm so thankful for Your mercy—but You know that sometimes I struggle to show mercy to others. I especially struggle to be merciful when I see someone making the same mistake or committing the same sin over and over and over again. But right now I pray that You would make me like You. Help me show Your mercy to everyone—with no exceptions.

EVENING

HEART GUARD

Be anxious for nothing, but in everything by prayer and supplication, with thanksgiving, let your requests be made known to God; and the peace of God, which surpasses all understanding, will guard your hearts and minds through Christ Jesus.

PHILIPPIANS 4:6–7 NKJV

When my heart is hurting, I should pray, Lord. How often do I remember that—or feel like praying when my mind is distracted? Help me to allow Your Spirit to calm my thoughts and comfort my heart. I need Your peace to guard me day by day.

DAY 191

MORNING

CHEERFULNESS

"Be of good cheer, daughter."
MATTHEW 9:22 NKJV

Jesus, I can't imagine You as a solemn man. I believe You enjoyed life a lot, and I know You brought joy to those around You. Why else would sinners and tax collectors want to eat with You (as Your enemies pointed out)? Help me pattern my daily attitude after Your example and heed Your command to "be of good cheer." Let me reflect You in the way I live. Amen.

EVENING

THE FIRST PRIORITY

" 'Love the Lord your God with all your heart and with all your soul and with all your mind.' This is the first and greatest commandment."
MATTHEW 22:37–38 NIV

Father, You are my everything! Without You, I wouldn't be here. Forgive me for allowing so many other things to squeeze between me and You. Help me not skip time with You, because it's so important to me! I never want to take our relationship for granted.

MORNING

LIVING IN THE NOW

"Forget the former things; do not dwell on the past. See, I am doing a new thing! Now it springs up; do you not perceive it?"

ISAIAH 43:18–19 NIV

I can't change the past, Lord, but I think about it a lot. It's a waste of time, and I hate when my mind goes there. Lord, help me focus on today. Help me keep my attention on the priorities You've given me. Help me live in the present. Show me what I can do today to make an eternal difference.

EVENING

STANDING ON MY FEET

"But rise and stand on your feet; for I have appeared to you for this purpose, to make you a minister and a witness."

ACTS 26:16 NKJV

Dear Lord, I've depended a lot on the faith and Bible knowledge of people around me instead of developing my own. When I stand in front of You, You'll see only *me*, and I so want to hear You say, "Well done." Please increase my faith and devotion to You, Father. Amen.

DAY 193

MORNING

SHIELDED

Most important of all, you need a covering of faith in front of you. This is to put out the fire-arrows of the devil.

EPHESIANS 6:16 NLV

Lord, You tell me that my faith is a shield that will protect me from evil. Reinforce that shield today. Make my faith greater and stronger so I'll be ready when I go through difficult times—when Satan is shooting his fiery darts at me. I won't be afraid, Lord, because I'm standing on Your promises.

EVENING

WHEN OTHERS LET YOU DOWN

Make allowance for each other's faults, and forgive anyone who offends you. Remember, the Lord forgave you, so you must forgive others.

COLOSSIANS 3:13 NLT

When people in my life fail me, Lord, I can't help but feel unimportant. Remind me of those times when things happened that were out of my control and I ended up disappointing someone myself. Fill me with compassion and understanding for others. Help me get over any frustration I feel and show them Your love.

MORNING

JUST JESUS

They replied, "Believe in the Lord Jesus, and you will be saved—you and your household."
ACTS 16:31 NIV

Father God, I'm always amazed that Your gospel is so simple: Believe in the Lord Jesus. Be saved. That's it. It's not a mysterious formula. It's not some unattainable level of enlightenment. It's not dressing a certain way. It's not a thousand-mile pilgrimage. It's just Jesus. Help me stay true to this message by staying close to You. Amen.

EVENING

THE WAY OF PEACE

The fruit of that righteousness will be peace; its effect will be quietness and confidence forever.
ISAIAH 32:17 NIV

Because I believe in You, Lord, You grow spiritual fruit in my life—things like peace. You promise I can live in quietness and confidence *forever*! Thank You for Your faithfulness to me. Whenever I can't see the path ahead, You point me in the right direction, establishing me in Your way of peace.

DAY 195

MORNING

GOD'S GENTLENESS

"You have also given me the shield of Your salvation; Your gentleness has made me great."

2 SAMUEL 22:36 NKJV

Father God, when I think about Your gift of salvation, I'm so grateful for the amazing grace You have shown me. But there's another side to Your salvation. Lord, I'm thankful for Your gentleness that makes me strong enough to face every trouble. Because You have saved me, I never need to be afraid.

EVENING

A RENEWED ATTITUDE

Let the Spirit renew your thoughts and attitudes. Put on your new nature, created to be like God—truly righteous and holy.

EPHESIANS 4:23–24 NLT

Lord, please change the way I think about my time and how I use it. Every day, things are continually in my face, screaming for my attention, while other things—more important things like the feelings and needs of those around me—tend to slip into the background. Help me realize that my time spent focusing on eternal things is not so much a sacrifice as a reward.

MORNING

A GENTLE AND QUIET SPIRIT

The unfading beauty of a gentle and quiet spirit. . .is of great worth in God's sight.

1 PETER 3:4 NIV

Father God, I read in the Bible that You value a spirit that is gentle and quiet. Cultivating this kind of spirit is so hard for me! I have my own opinions about things. Sometimes I struggle to keep quiet or speak softly. Yet, Lord, You know I want to be that way. Please teach me how to be quiet and gentle. Amen.

EVENING

THE RIGHT TIME

We humans keep brainstorming options and plans, but GOD's purpose prevails.

PROVERBS 19:21 MSG

Father God, there is so much I want to do, but I just don't know when to do it. Your timing is everything. You've planned out each one of my steps. You know the way I should go. Help me trust in Your purpose. Give me confidence to know when it's time to step forward. Thank You for causing everything to happen in Your time, not mine.

DAY 197

MORNING

GOD'S ARMOR

But let us who live in the light be clearheaded, protected by the armor of faith and love, and wearing as our helmet the confidence of our salvation.

1 THESSALONIANS 5:8 NLT

Lord, remind me not to go out into life's temptations and trials without first putting on Your armor. Teach me to grab hold of these gifts and harness the power You offer through them. Give me the opportunity to use Your armor to bless others, protecting them against evil.

EVENING

WONDERFUL WORKS

He has made His wonderful works to be remembered; the LORD is gracious and full of compassion.

PSALM 111:4 NKJV

Father God, the world becomes tiny if I focus on my own pain. I'm thankful You've given me so many wonderful things to remind me of Your grace and compassion. You love all Your kids, including me. I know You have many more works to do in my life. Keep my eyes open for them as I stick close to You.

MORNING

THE ALREADY-DONE LIST

The Lord came to us from far away, saying, "I have loved you with a love that lasts forever. So I have helped you come to Me with loving-kindness."

JEREMIAH 31:3 NLV

Dear Lord, I know I often base my self-worth on how much I've accomplished. Help me remember that I can never *do* enough to earn Your love. I'm already loved, completely and eternally. The only thing that really needed doing, You did on the cross. Thank You, Jesus.

EVENING

UNMET EXPECTATIONS

Let us hold on to the hope we say we have and not be changed. We can trust God that He will do what He promised.

HEBREWS 10:23 NLV

Lord, my expectations were high, and I'm so disappointed that things aren't working out as I'd hoped. Help me remember that You're in control. I give this situation to You, knowing You *always* keep Your promises. Things might not look like what I expected, but I'm learning that Your way is always better in the end.

DAY 199

MORNING

QUIET-TIME QUEST

"In quietness and trust is your strength."
ISAIAH 30:15 NIV

Father God, You know how much I love spending time with my friends. I need Your help to enjoy solitude too. Let me see the value of spending some time alone so I can refresh my spirit and worship You without noise. Help me plan times of quietness in my day, away from my phone and all the other distractions. Help me make quiet times my quest. Amen.

EVENING

PURSUING THE PRIZE

I press toward the goal for the prize of the upward call of God in Christ Jesus.
PHILIPPIANS 3:14 NKJV

Heavenly Father, Jesus knew His mission while He was here on earth, and He completed it. Give me the same drive and power to accomplish my mission. I'm committed and ready to pursue whatever You call me to do. Thank You for the courage to move forward. I'm stepping out in faith, trusting You to lead me.

DAY 200

MORNING

LIT

"Be dressed ready for service and keep your lamps burning."
LUKE 12:35 NIV

Lord, You've promised to come back to earth one day; and when You do, I want to be ready. Keep me ready to serve You all the days before then too. Everywhere I look, I can see darkness. Please, Lord, turn on the lights in my heart. Show me ways to share Your light with everyone around me, pushing back against the darkness with Your brilliance!

EVENING

JESUS' EXAMPLE

If we confess our sins, he is faithful and just and will forgive us our sins and purify us from all unrighteousness.
1 JOHN 1:9 NIV

When I think about forgiveness, I think about You, Jesus. Help me reflect Your love by forgiving the people who wrong me. Sometimes I want revenge. But through the power of Your Spirit inside me, I will follow Your example. Forgive me for all my sins, Lord, and help me to walk in Your ways.

DAY 201

MORNING

WIDE AWAKE

Keep awake! Do not sleep like others. Watch and keep your minds awake to what is happening.

1 THESSALONIANS 5:6 NLV

You know how tired I am, Lord. You know how worn out I've become facing troubles and challenges lately. Help me not to give in to my exhaustion. Please send godly friends into my life who can encourage me to keep on the path You've laid out for Your kids. Keep me wide awake and alert, focused always on You. Amen.

EVENING

SEE IT THROUGH

The ways of right-living people glow with light; the longer they live, the brighter they shine.

PROVERBS 4:18 MSG

Lord, my life isn't turning out like I thought it would. You never said life would be easy, but You have promised to do more than I can imagine. Help me see my dream through to reality. Show me what it looks like from Your perspective. Help me rise to whatever heights You want me to reach.

DAY 202

MORNING

REMOVING THE LIMITS

Listen to my voice in the morning, LORD. Each morning I bring my requests to you and wait expectantly.

PSALM 5:3 NLT

Lord, You've promised to hear me when I pray and to honor me as I serve You. Right now I'm removing the limits that have held me back. It doesn't matter what other people think; I won't let them discourage me. My heart is tuned to Your voice, and I hear Your words. Nothing is impossible with You.

EVENING

WHENEVER WE CRY OUT

"Then you call on the name of your god,
and I will call on the name of the LORD.
The god who answers by fire—he is God."

1 KINGS 18:24 NIV

Lord, there is never a time I cry out to You when You are not instantly listening. You're never too busy to pay attention to me, and You're always powerful enough to answer. You are the God who answered Elijah by fire! Hear and answer me in amazing ways, I pray.

MORNING

RESCUED!

The LORD says, "I will rescue those who love me.
I will protect those who trust in my name."
PSALM 91:14 NLT

When troubles threaten to drown me, Lord, reach down and save me. Deliver me from the floods. Rescue me from the fire. Remove me from the storm. Protect me from the violence. Pick me up and set me on a high place where I will be safe next to You. I know my Deliverer is coming. Amen.

EVENING

NEEDING ENCOURAGEMENT

May our Lord Jesus Christ himself and God our Father, who loved us and by his grace gave us eternal encouragement and good hope, encourage your hearts and strengthen you in every good deed and word.
2 THESSALONIANS 2:16–17 NIV

Lord, please encourage my heart and strengthen me in everything I say and do. I need Your truth to lift my spirit. Give me the energy and grit I need to keep going even when I'm tired.

MORNING

BLESSED ARE THE FLEXIBLE

This is the day the LORD has made;
we will rejoice and be glad in it.
PSALM 118:24 NKJV

Father God, I don't like interruptions in my routine. They make me feel flustered and uneasy. But sometimes You have to reorganize for me, because I haven't noticed where You've been directing me. Or maybe there's someone You need me to meet or a disaster You want me to avoid. Please help me be flexible, aware that You're ruling over everything.

EVENING

A COMPASSIONATE HEART

Blessed be the God and Father of our Lord Jesus Christ,
the Father of mercies and God of all comfort.
2 CORINTHIANS 1:3 NKJV

Lord, You love us so much. Fill me with Your love until it overflows. Give me a compassionate heart that longs to help people. Show me where I can help, whether at a soup kitchen, my school, my church, or wherever. Lead me as I pray for others and for Your help.

DAY 205

MORNING

PRESERVED

The LORD preserves all who love Him.

PSALM 145:20 NKJV

Preserve me, dear Lord. Keep me safe—that's what I'm asking You to do. There is so much I need preserving from. Guard my physical body, my mind, and my heart. Watch over me as I move from place to place, activity to activity. Take away my worries, my fears, and my troubles. I love You—and I need Your help now. Thank You for never leaving me alone. Amen.

EVENING

PERSEVERANCE IN PRAYER

As you know, we count as blessed those who have persevered. You have heard of Job's perseverance and have seen what the Lord finally brought about. The Lord is full of compassion and mercy.

JAMES 5:11 NIV

I feel like I've been praying forever for a situation that doesn't seem to be changing, Lord. I know You're in control. You know all things. So one more time, I lift up my concerns to You, confident You'll handle things in the best way.

MORNING

LIES

If we confess our sins to him, he is faithful and just to forgive us our sins and to cleanse us from all wickedness.

1 JOHN 1:9 NLT

Father God, someone lied to me today. Then I realized that the burden had become mine because I didn't let it go. A lie that someone else told became anger and resentment in my heart. Show me how to lay ugly things at the foot of the cross and pick up joy instead.

EVENING

BLESSING MY ENEMIES

Bless your enemies; no cursing under your breath.

ROMANS 12:14 MSG

Father God, I pray that You'll bless those who haven't been kind to me. You know who they are. Help me forgive other people like You always forgive me. Help me to repay evil not with evil but with good, because that's what You do. Give me the strength to be kind to my enemies, even helpful, and to keep anger out of my heart.

DAY 207

MORNING

OUR HEAVENLY HOMELAND

They agreed that they were foreigners and nomads here on earth. Obviously people who say such things are looking forward to a country they can call their own.

HEBREWS 11:13–14 NLT

Father God, heaven is an actual place, as real as this earth. When I live as if this earth is the ultimate goal, I tend to be selfish. But when I remember that heaven is my real destination, I value the lasting things. And that's what I want to do.

EVENING

HELPING THE HUNGRY

"For I was hungry and you gave me something to eat, I was thirsty and you gave me something to drink."

MATTHEW 25:35 NIV

Lord, people are hungry all over the world; they're hungry even right here where I live. You taught Your followers that whenever they helped someone in need, they were helping You. Show me where I can use my hands to help. I want to serve others in Your name, Jesus. Amen.

MORNING

THE ONE NEEDFUL THING

I will be fully satisfied as with the richest of foods;
with singing lips my mouth will praise you.
PSALM 63:5 NIV

Father God, You are the giver of good gifts, and You give generously. But I confess—I'm often on the lookout for more. Thank You for the things I have, and help me control my desire for more. No *thing* I have will make me complete. Only You can make me complete, Lord. You are what I need.

EVENING

A NEIGHBORHOOD PRAYER

We do not use those things to fight with that the world uses.
We use the things God gives to fight with and they have power.
2 CORINTHIANS 10:4 NLV

Father God, my neighborhood isn't perfect. Help me remember that nothing can be made perfect without Your divine power. Be with me and my family as we take a walk and pray for each family living here. May our prayers serve as a weapon to fight the bad and usher in the good.

MORNING

ALIVE AND BLESSED

The LORD protects and preserves them—
they are counted among the blessed in the land—
he does not give them over to the desire of their foes.
PSALM 41:2 NIV

This world is full of dangers, isn't it, Lord? But I don't want to live a life of fear, and You don't want me to either. You call me to be bold and fearless. Thank You that You've promised not only to save my life but to bless me too.

EVENING

COMFORT THE SUFFERING

[Jesus said,] "You are the light of the world—
like a city on a hilltop that cannot be hidden."
MATTHEW 5:14 NLT

Jesus, I pray for Your bright light to spread out into the world, for Your love to reach the ends of the earth. Please comfort those who suffer. Heal them and guard them. Let them know You're there. And let me know how I can help. How can I be a light in this world?

MORNING

THE PERFECTIONIST TRAP

"God's way is perfect."
2 SAMUEL 22:31 NLT

Lord, I'm so glad You're a holy, perfect, and separate God. We could never make a god like You. I would never bow to Artemis or Baal or Thor; but I've realized that in my perfectionism, I'm setting up another god to worship—myself. Always doing, always perfecting, always tweaking my little universe. Please help me be content with imperfection. Only You are perfect, and I'm complete in You.

EVENING

BLESSED!

"Blessed are those whose transgressions are forgiven, whose sins are covered."
ROMANS 4:7 NIV

Because of You, Jesus, I'm blessed. I'm forgiven. No matter what I experience any day of my life, Your blessings stay the same. You don't change Your mind and decide not to love or forgive me. Thank You for covering my flaws and failures, because I need this gift every single day. Your complete forgiveness of my sin is the most important gift I'll ever receive.

DAY 211

MORNING

NEVER FORSAKEN

For the LORD loves justice, and does not forsake His saints; they are preserved forever.

PSALM 37:28 NKJV

Father God, I've been abandoned in my life. Friends have deserted me, leaving me feeling empty and alone and helpless. Thank You that You'll never forsake me; You'll never abandon me. I'm grateful for the security of that promise. You'll keep me safe forever in Your loving arms, which are more than strong enough to hold me and all my problems.

EVENING

HOW CAN I SERVE?

Don't act thoughtlessly, but understand what the Lord wants you to do.

EPHESIANS 5:17 NLT

Lord, I'm looking for direction. I'm not sure how You want me to serve You. So often I feel incapable or untalented, as if others could do things much better than I ever could. But I know those feelings aren't from You. Help me understand what You want me to do. And as I do it, I won't worry about pleasing others, only about pleasing You.

MORNING

JUST DO IT

But be doers of the word, and not hearers only, deceiving yourselves.
JAMES 1:22 NKJV

Lord, please give me an obedient heart. Sometimes I find myself putting off what You're telling me to do. Either I don't trust You or I want my own way, and neither of those things is good. Help me obey because I know that You're right and that I can trust You. Help me do what You say every time You speak to me.

EVENING

CLOTHED IN GOD'S WARDROBE

Therefore, as God's chosen people, holy and dearly loved, clothe yourselves with compassion, kindness, humility, gentleness and patience.
COLOSSIANS 3:12 NIV

Father God, help me remember as I get dressed tomorrow that the most important clothes I put on aren't in my closet. They're things like compassion, kindness, humility, gentleness, and patience. When I'm "wearing" these qualities, there will be no doubt that I'm Your daughter. People will see You in me! And that's the best kind of compliment.

MORNING

SAVED FROM ALL EVIL

The LORD keeps you from all harm
and watches over your life.
PSALM 121:7 NLT

Lord, evil comes in so many shapes and forms. Sometimes it comes into my life disguised; and by the time I recognize it's there, I'm already in danger. When this happens, please be my rescuer (even when I don't ask for rescuing!). Thank You that You're always watching over me and will protect me from every kind of evil.

EVENING

BOLD AND DILIGENT

"Be bold and diligent. And GOD be
with you as you do your best."
2 CHRONICLES 19:11 MSG

Father God, I want to do my best, knowing You're with me all the way. Help me to be brave. Help me not to panic. Neither fear nor anxiety is from You. I need to focus on You to build up my faith and my confidence. I'm ready to listen to Your voice. Lead me, Lord, where You want me to go.

MORNING

MY HIDING PLACE

You are my hiding place; you will protect me from trouble and surround me with songs of deliverance.
PSALM 32:7 NIV

Heavenly Father, when troubles rush at me no matter which direction I turn, be my hiding place. When I run into Your arms, wrap me up in Your embrace and sing to me Your sweet song of deliverance. May I never think I'm so self-sufficient that I reject Your comfort and protection.

EVENING

IN HIS STRENGTH

I can do all things because Christ gives me the strength.
PHILIPPIANS 4:13 NLV

What an amazing thought—I can do all things through You, Lord! You give me the power, the energy, the ways and means! Here in Your presence, I can feel the power of Your love. Please fill me with Your strength so I can accomplish all You want me to do. Plant the words "I can do all things through Christ—He strengthens me!" in my heart forever. Amen.

MORNING

JUST FOR ME

Then I can answer anyone who taunts me,
for I trust in your word.
PSALM 119:42 NIV

Lord, I pray for insight as I read the Bible. I want to know You better today than I did yesterday, and better tomorrow than I do today, so that I can stand confidently in Your Word. Thank You for the verses I'll read today and for the way they'll speak to me, as if You wrote them just for me this morning.

EVENING

HONORING OTHERS WITH MY MOUTH

Don't try to impress others. Be humble,
thinking of others as better than yourselves.
PHILIPPIANS 2:3 NLT

Lord, sometimes I'm tempted to shout my own praises. Instead, please use my words to honor people, not impress them. I want to lift people up, not bring them down. Give me a good attitude, positive words, and encouraging comments. Guard my mouth; and when You need to, put Your hand over it to keep it shut.

MORNING

THE SIMPLE LIFE

Aspire to lead a quiet life, to mind your own business, and to work with your own hands.

1 THESSALONIANS 4:11 NKJV

Father God, I hear people talk about a "simpler" life. And sometimes that sounds good to me. My life can be pretty complex! My spiritual life could use a little simplifying too. Help me concentrate on one or two verses each day. Help me keep simple goals and a simple faith as I simply live for You. Amen.

EVENING

PATH OF BLESSING

All the paths of the Lord are loving and true for those who keep His agreement and keep His Laws.

PSALM 25:10 NLV

How can I thank You for calling me to walk with You, Jesus? While obeying You challenges me sometimes, so many blessings come from doing Your will. Even when I fail, Your mercy draws me back to Your way because Your love is unfailing. I never want to wander from Your side, Lord!

DAY 217

MORNING

A TOWER ON A ROCK

The God of my rock; in him will I trust: he is my shield, and the horn of my salvation, my high tower, and my refuge.

2 Samuel 22:3 KJV

You, Lord, are my place of absolute safety: a high tower built on a rock that will never move. When troubles and temptations surround me, teach me to look up. Help me look above everything else and see You—and then run to You as fast as I can!

EVENING

SHELTER IN HIM

Those who live in the shelter of the Most High will find rest in the shadow of the Almighty.

Psalm 91:1 NLT

Father God, I don't want to just visit Your shelter; I want to live there! Peace, love, and harmony fill my life when I stand by Your side. You give me every good thing, simply for sticking close to You. May I always find my rest in You, Lord. May I make my home in Your shelter.

MORNING

MIRROR, MIRROR

Thank you for making me so wonderfully complex!
Your workmanship is marvelous—how well I know it.
PSALM 139:14 NLT

Father, when I look at certain people, all I see is how much I don't measure up. They seem naturally kinder, more confident, prettier. I spend more time thinking about how other people see me than about how You see me. Yet You made me for Your purposes. Help me trust You and trust that I'm wonderfully made!

EVENING

PERSONAL GRACE

But to each one of us grace has
been given as Christ apportioned it.
EPHESIANS 4:7 NIV

You've given me just the right amount of grace, Lord. No matter what I'm doing today, You give grace to cover all my needs. No matter what my situation, You help me. Nothing in my life is so awful that You can't bring a blessing from it if I seek Your will. Thank You for loving me so much. Help me do Your will today.

DAY 219

MORNING

THE PATH TO JOY

Keep your lives free from the love of money
and be content with what you have.
HEBREWS 13:5 NIV

Lord, wherever I look, I see ads. It's hard to be content when I'm bombarded with messages that say I should want more. I know that getting more and more stuff isn't the path to joy. Let my life be marked by a deep contentment that starts in You, the reason for my joy. In Jesus' name. Amen.

EVENING

WORLDLY FEARS

"Blessed is the one who trusts in the LORD,
whose confidence is in him."
JEREMIAH 17:7 NIV

Lord, I'm so blessed! Even though I'm feeling uncertain about some things right now, I trust in You. I refuse to go along with the world, pushed forward by fear and insecurity. I won't bow to outside pressures. I'll put my confidence in You because I trust You to look out for me and always be with me, no matter what.

MORNING

MY REFUGE

The LORD also will be a refuge for the oppressed, a refuge in times of trouble.

PSALM 9:9 KJV

In times of trouble, Lord, when the pressure is just too much, thank You that You're my refuge—a place of peace, love, and acceptance. Teach me to seek Your protection at the beginning of troubles rather than trying to handle them on my own. I don't get extra points for trying to manage all by myself.

EVENING

GIVING FORGIVENESS

"For if you forgive other people when they sin against you, your heavenly Father will also forgive you."

MATTHEW 6:14 NIV

Lord, because You've forgiven me, You also expect me to forgive. You don't want me to hold on to the wrongs of others while being forgiven myself. You tell me to take Your love as an example for my life. Please give me compassion for everyone who hurts me, Lord. Help me love them as You've loved me.

DAY 221

MORNING

THE MISSING PIECE

When you have Christ, you are complete.
COLOSSIANS 2:10 NLV

Lord, the people who still need You don't usually go around with "Unsaved" printed on their T-shirts. Sometimes they look just fine, like they aren't missing anything at all. Lord, this is when I'm really not sure how to tell them about You. I need Your help. Unbelievers are incomplete, despite the way they might look. I trust You to lead me because You love them so much. Amen.

EVENING

UNDER CONTROL

Blessed are those whose help is the God of Jacob, whose hope is in the LORD their God. He is the Maker of heaven and earth, the sea, and everything in them—he remains faithful forever.
PSALM 146:5–6 NIV

Lord, You faithfully control everything in this world. Looking at Your creation, I see Your hand in every detail. When I need You, You're there. Thank You, Lord, for all Your blessings. Keep me mindful of them.

MORNING

TIME MANAGEMENT

Teach us to number our days,
that we may gain a heart of wisdom.
PSALM 90:12 NIV

Father God, so often I seem to run out of time to do my homework and chores. Life was a lot easier when I was a little kid and didn't have so many responsibilities. I'm having trouble getting everything done. Please help me, Lord. Teach me to manage my time wisely. Show me how to make the most of my days.

EVENING

HELD BY HIM

The LORD directs the steps of the godly. He delights
in every detail of their lives. Though they stumble,
they will never fall, for the LORD holds them by the hand.
PSALM 37:23–24 NLT

Lord, I may stumble, but I'll never fall flat on my face when I'm living life with You! I'm only human; sometimes I make mistakes. But even then, You don't desert me. When I'm held up by You, I have nothing to fear. Thank You!

DAY 223

MORNING

A SONG IN MY HEART

But I will sing of Your power; yes, I will sing aloud of Your mercy in the morning; for You have been my defense and refuge in the day of my trouble.

PSALM 59:16 NKJV

Father God, I'm going to start today singing. Give me a song about Your power and mercy that will stay with me all day long, especially when the stresses come. No matter what life throws at me, I want to live with that song in my heart.

EVENING

ONE SAVIOR

"He is the one all the prophets testified about, saying that everyone who believes in him will have their sins forgiven through his name."

ACTS 10:43 NLT

No one else can forgive sin like You do, Jesus. People can help me or hurt me, but that will never change the fact that I'm saved. You've freed me from sin! Nothing on earth gives that kind of freedom. Let nothing on earth keep me from believing in You, my Savior.

MORNING

NEED HOPE?

You are my hiding place and my shield; I hope in Your word.
PSALM 119:114 NKJV

Father God, if I'm low on hope, all I have to do is open the Bible. There I learn that You formed me before I was born, that You love me, that You provided a way for me to have a relationship with You through Jesus, and that You have amazing plans for me here and in heaven. Your Word fills me with amazing hope!

EVENING

FEARING GOD

"He shows mercy from generation to generation to all who fear him."
LUKE 1:50 NLT

God, I know fearing You doesn't mean being afraid of You. It means I'm in awe of You and respect You because of who You are—God Almighty. Thank You that Your mercy will follow me and all my family members who believe in Jesus. No matter what we're going through now, we can trust You completely. Please show us Your mercy every day!

DAY 225

MORNING

MY PRAYER WARRIORS

He is always wrestling in prayer for you, that you may stand firm in all the will of God, mature and fully assured.

COLOSSIANS 4:12 NIV

I thank You, Lord, for all the people who have prayed for me. They've lifted me up to You faithfully and passionately. I ask You to bless them today. Strengthen their faith in the invisible power of their prayers. Please bring me to their minds today, Lord, because I need their prayers.

EVENING

FAITHFUL LORD

But the Lord is faithful, who will establish you and guard you from the evil one.

2 THESSALONIANS 3:3 NKJV

I've felt the devil's attacks, Lord. His traps have caught me in sin, and his sneak attacks have tried to lure me away from You. But Satan is a defeated enemy. When I'm strong in You, he cannot get past Your guard. Your strength always defends me. Thank You for protecting me, Lord. No battle that You fight is ever lost.

MORNING

SAFE IN THE MIDST OF THE WORLD

"I do not ask You to take them out of the world.
I ask You to keep them from the devil."
JOHN 17:15 NLV

Jesus, You didn't ask that I be physically removed from the earth so that I'd be immune to the world's temptations and tests. Instead, You asked that God would protect me no matter what I face. Thank You, Jesus, that You prayed for *me*. Thank You for keeping me safe.

EVENING

PERFECTION AND PEACE

Mark the perfect man, and behold the upright:
for the end of that man is peace.
PSALM 37:37 KJV

Everyone wants peace, Lord. I try to live peacefully with others, but it's not always easy. This verse seems to say that perfection leads to peace, but that sounds impossible. Lord, You're not saying we'll never make mistakes. You're saying that as we grow in maturity and follow Your ways diligently, Your peace will be the result.

DAY 227

MORNING

THE UNVEILING

So all of us who have had that veil removed can see and reflect the glory of the Lord. And the Lord—who is the Spirit—makes us more and more like him as we are changed into his glorious image.

2 CORINTHIANS 3:18 NLT

Jesus, You've made a way for me to not be separated from God anymore. And now Your Spirit is making me more like You. Eventually, this transformation will be finished—I can't wait for the final unveiling!

EVENING

ONE REQUIREMENT

For God so loved the world that he gave his one and only Son, that whoever believes in him shall not perish but have eternal life.

JOHN 3:16 NIV

Can it be so simple, Lord? I just have to believe? Yes! You promise that faith by itself opens the door to eternal life. I don't have to jump through hoops to earn Your love. You gave Your Son so that we can spend forever with You. I'm so thankful!

MORNING

YES AND NO

"All you need to say is simply 'Yes' or 'No'; anything beyond this comes from the evil one."
MATTHEW 5:37 NIV

Father God, please keep teaching me Your ways so that no evil will take root in my life. Remind me to make my word count so that my "yes" means yes and my "no" means no. Make me a person others can trust. When people ask me why I do what I do, let me always point them to You.

EVENING

MOVING MOUNTAINS

"For sure, I tell you, a person may say to this mountain, 'Move from here into the sea.' And if he does not doubt, but believes that what he says will be done, it will happen."
MARK 11:23 NLV

The mountains in my life aren't made of dirt and rock, Lord. They're made of doubts and fears, but they're still real. Help my doubting heart. Keep my eyes on You. Remind me that no mountain is big to You.

DAY 229

MORNING

NEVER THIRSTY

"Whoever drinks the water I give them will never thirst. Indeed, the water I give them will become in them a spring of water welling up to eternal life."

JOHN 4:14 NIV

Lord, I have to drink water every day, or I'll get really, really thirsty. Thank You for the promise that I never need to be spiritually thirsty again when I've believed and trusted in You. You've put a spring of water in my heart. Your Spirit quenches my thirst—forever!

EVENING

SHINING ALL NIGHT

She sees that what she has earned is good.
Her lamp does not go out at night.

PROVERBS 31:18 NLV

Lord, the light of Your Spirit never goes out, no matter what's going on in my life. Remind me that Your faithfulness and love never fail. Lord, thank You for lighting my way into the future. Darkness and difficulties may surround me, but I know Your light is shining all through the night. Please keep my heart faithful.

MORNING

BACK TO CENTER

Walk straight ahead so the weak leg will not be turned aside, but will be healed.

HEBREWS 12:13 NLV

Father God, I need balance in my life. I'm so prone to lopsidedness—to extremes. Staying centered is challenging. I need You to straighten me out and keep me on Your narrow way. In those areas of my life where I'm leaning to the side, please bring me back to center. In Jesus' name I pray. Amen.

EVENING

A FRIEND OF JESUS

"You are my friends if you do what I command."

JOHN 15:14 NLT

How do I show that I'm Your friend, Lord? You tell me right here: My obedience shows I really love You. I need to put belief into action. Living faithfully during trials is hard, Lord, but it also draws me close to You. Our friendship grows through my problems as I experience Your trustworthiness. Help me obey You always. You are my best friend, Lord.

DAY 231

MORNING

A TIME FOR EVERYTHING

There is a time for everything, and a season for every activity under the heavens.

ECCLESIASTES 3:1 NIV

Father, my day is packed! I have three tests at school, practice after school, and then homework after that. Help me take things one by one. Jesus was never rushing. He had time to pray on a mountain, chat beside a well, and cook fish with His friends—all while doing Your will. Show me the right time for everything.

EVENING

A HELPING HAND

"When you give to the needy, do not let your left hand know what your right hand is doing, so that your giving may be in secret. Then your Father, who sees what is done in secret, will reward you."

MATTHEW 6:3–4 NIV

Lord, so many people in this world are needy. Show me where I can give. Use my abilities to help. But always keep me humble. Giving is about helping. Giving is about You, not me.

MORNING

HOPE TO THE END

So prepare your minds for action and exercise self-control. Put all your hope in the gracious salvation that will come to you when Jesus Christ is revealed to the world.

1 PETER 1:13 NLT

I've put all my hope in You, Lord Jesus. Your death and resurrection have saved me for all of eternity. I want to live like You did. I want to follow Your example now, in my everyday life. Help me always keep You in focus.

EVENING

HE GIVES ME STRENGTH!

To You, O my Strength, I will sing praises; for God is my defense, my God of mercy.

PSALM 59:17 NKJV

Father God, when I feel weak, Your strength upholds me. When I feel afraid, Your courage emboldens me. When I feel down, Your presence lifts me. You are always there for me. How great, how wonderful, how amazing You are, my God, my friend, my Father! I'm here before You, singing endless praises to Your name!

MORNING

HOSPITALITY

Cheerfully share your home with those who need a meal or a place to stay.
1 PETER 4:9 NLT

Lord, I don't always enjoy having people over to my house. Sometimes I just want to take it easy and not have to be polite and helpful. But You want me to be welcoming to people. Because You have blessed me, You want me to share with others. Lord, please change my attitude and my heart. Amen.

EVENING

PRAISE TO MY CREATOR

Bless the LORD, O my soul! O LORD my God, You are very great: You are clothed with honor and majesty, who cover Yourself with light as with a garment, who stretch out the heavens like a curtain.
PSALM 104:1–2 NKJV

Father God, You made the planets, the stars, the oceans, and the land. Your creative abilities are amazing! You are wrapped in light, Lord, and I come into that light now to be close to You and to praise Your holy name.

MORNING

A FIRM PLACE

But the Lord is faithful, who will establish you and guard you from the evil one.

2 THESSALONIANS 3:3 NKJV

Father God, I know You're faithful. Be my rock, a firm place for me to stand, the foundation of my entire life. Make me firm and solid too, so I can always resist evil. And as my faith develops and matures, please help me lead others to find their strength in You. We all need You, Lord!

EVENING

ENEMIES SILENCED BY PRAISE

Out of the mouth of children and babies, You have built up strength because of those who hate You, and to quiet those who fight against You.

PSALM 8:2 NLV

Father God, You hold the heavens in Your hands. You hold up the entire universe! Thank You so much that You are on my side so I don't have to be afraid of people who want to harm me or of the devil who dogs my steps. My enemies are silenced when I praise You!

DAY 235

MORNING

LOVE'S BEACON

No one has seen God at any time. If we love one another, God abides in us, and His love has been perfected in us.

1 JOHN 4:12 NKJV

Lord, You know how selfishness, hurt feelings, and laziness can mess up friendships. You know how I sometimes act when no one is watching. But I love You, and You are still teaching me how to love. Increase my love, Lord. Let it shine out for everyone around to see. Amen.

EVENING

SET FREE BY THE TRUTH

To the Jews who had believed him, Jesus said, "If you hold to my teaching, you are really my disciples. Then you will know the truth, and the truth will set you free."

JOHN 8:31–32 NIV

Lord, for so long, sin held me tight. I tried to change, but I was powerless. I couldn't break free on my own. Then You rescued me! Your love and strength empowered me, Lord. Now I choose to follow Your way. Your truth has set me free!

DAY 236

MORNING

NO SLIPPING

He will not allow your foot to be moved;
He who keeps you will not slumber.
PSALM 121:3 NKJV

Father God, I'm coming to a place in my life where the road looks slippery and dangerous ahead. Please hold my hand, Lord; and when I need You to, please pick me up and carry me. I know You'll never leave me or even take a break to get some rest. Thank You that I can trust You, even on difficult stretches of the path.

EVENING

CHANGE ME, LORD

Yet you, LORD, are our Father. We are the clay,
you are the potter; we are all the work of your hand.
ISAIAH 64:8 NIV

Lord, You know my past, present, and future. You're the potter and I'm the clay, the work of Your hands. As You reshape my life, molding me into the girl You want me to be, help me trust Your wisdom. I want to be a vessel sturdy enough to hold all Your love.

DAY 237

MORNING

THE REAL ME

I have chosen the way of truth.

PSALM 119:30 NKJV

Heavenly Father, a lot of people in my world are posers. They're afraid to be real with others—to show who they really are. Oddly enough, sometimes we're afraid to be real even with You—and You know everything about us anyway. I want to be genuine with others, including You. Give me the courage to reject "being perfect" and to live out my life and relationships in an authentic way.

EVENING

GIVER OF GOOD THINGS

To the person who pleases him, God gives wisdom, knowledge and happiness.

ECCLESIASTES 2:26 NIV

Father God, You're the giver of all good things—things like wisdom and knowledge and happiness. Tonight I'm especially grateful that You've given me happiness. I'm totally undeserving of Your blessing but also totally thankful it's mine. I want to bring You joy as I follow Your ways and serve the people around me. Knowing that I'm pleasing You—that in itself is a blessing too.

MORNING

CHAOS!

You will keep in perfect peace all who trust in you, all whose thoughts are fixed on you!
ISAIAH 26:3 NLT

Father God, yesterday I was doing homework, texting my friends, and watching TV. After a while everything felt jumbled. It makes me wonder: How many of my crazy-feeling days are because I'm not centering my thoughts on You? You can keep me in perfect peace, Lord, so help me keep the chaos in check by spending more time with You.

EVENING

MOVING PAST MY MISTAKES

"The thief comes only to steal and kill and destroy; I have come that they may have life, and have it to the full."
JOHN 10:10 NIV

Lord, I can't erase my past, but You can—and have. Thank You for removing my sins and giving me a new life—a life I can live to the full. Help me to learn from the mistakes I've made and to move forward into the life You've planned for me.

MORNING

STRAIGHT WAYS

O Lord, lead me in what is right and good, because of the ones who hate me. Make Your way straight in front of me.

PSALM 5:8 NLV

Father God, sometimes I don't know which way I should go. Please show me clearly the way You want me to take. Remind me that You've already "been there, done that." I might question why we're going a certain direction, but You know what's best—and You have great plans for me.

EVENING

LET GO AND GRAB ON

My eyes are always on the LORD, for he rescues me from the traps of my enemies.

PSALM 25:15 NLT

Lord, I struggle to let go of things that are familiar, even when they're not good for me anymore. I need Your power to loosen my grip on the things I cling to so tightly. As I release them to You, please grant me courage to grab on to whatever You're waiting to give me.

MORNING

ACCOUNTABILITY

The LORD will be at your side and
will keep your foot from being snared.
PROVERBS 3:26 NIV

Lord, even really good people—people I look up to—sin. Thank You for reminding me that anyone, including me, is capable of any sin. And thank You for reminding me that You are there to protect us. Lord, surround me with people who will hold me accountable. I never want to let sin keep me from being totally useful to You. Amen.

EVENING

PURE-HEARTED FRIENDS

He who loves a pure heart and is kind in
his speaking has the king as his friend.
PROVERBS 22:11 NLV

Lord, when I'm going through tough times, You bring people into my life who offer me their friendship. Their pure hearts and kind words have comforted me and gotten me through. Thank You for their love—and thank You most of all that You are my best friend and stand by me in the darkest times.

MORNING

PLAIN PATHS

Teach me thy way, O LORD, and lead me in a plain path, because of mine enemies.

PSALM 27:11 KJV

I need Your help, Lord. I can't see which way to go. The paths ahead are all jumbled, and I'm confused. The devil—my worst enemy—has made things hard to see because he wants me to go the wrong way. Please, Lord, lead me. Make Your way plain. And remove any evil intended to stop me from walking that direction.

EVENING

HOPE AND A FUTURE

"For I know the plans I have for you," declares the LORD, "plans to prosper you and not to harm you, plans to give you hope and a future."

JEREMIAH 29:11 NIV

I don't always know how to make the best choices, Lord. But You see the big picture and want to direct me in the best way every single day. All I have to do is listen. Thank You, Lord, for planning my days and my future.

MORNING

WALKING IN TRUTH

Teach me Your way, O LORD; I will walk in Your truth; unite my heart to fear Your name.

PSALM 86:11 NKJV

I'm guilty of having a divided heart, Lord God. I want to do Your will, but I also want my will to be done. Forgive me for my selfishness. When my heart feels torn, Lord, please unite me so that I have a single focus in life: Your way, Your truth, Your will, Your path.

EVENING

PROTECTED

Give your burdens to the LORD, and he will take care of you. He will not permit the godly to slip and fall.

PSALM 55:22 NLT

Lord, I know nothing happens to me that You don't know about, and You're always looking out for me. Help me to keep believing in Your goodness no matter what I face. Thank You for taking my burdens and caring for me, Lord. In You, I am protected!

DAY 243

MORNING

POSTPONED DREAMS

He has made everything beautiful in its time.
ECCLESIASTES 3:11 NKJV

Lord, I have some dreams that I really, *really* want to come true. But it looks like at least one of them won't be happening anytime soon. Thank You for this verse. It's just what I need so I remember that You'll make everything beautiful at the right time—in Your time. I love You and trust You completely. Help me set my heart on You.

EVENING

GOD'S WATCHFUL CARE

The LORD watches over the foreigner and
sustains the fatherless and the widow,
but he frustrates the ways of the wicked.
PSALM 146:9 NIV

Lord, I'm so glad You watch over people who are left out by the world. When life feels unfair, I'm so glad to know You haven't left me. Right now, I'm feeling pretty powerless. Help me trust in You for my future. Thank You for caring about me so much. I need You, Lord. Amen.

MORNING

FRIENDS FOR EVERY TIME

There is a time to cry, and a time to laugh;
a time to have sorrow, and a time to dance.
ECCLESIASTES 3:4 NLV

Lord, I'm grateful for my friends. They're such a huge part of my life. When I need someone to vent to, they'll listen. When I need a kick to get me going, they'll kick! I can't imagine my life without them. Thank You for blessing me with friends. Help me be a good friend too.

EVENING

COVENANT OF LOVE

Know therefore that the LORD your God is God;
he is the faithful God, keeping his covenant of
love to a thousand generations of those who
love him and keep his commandments.
DEUTERONOMY 7:9 NIV

You're so faithful, Lord. Despite my mistakes, You want a relationship with me. Even when I go against Your Word, You encourage me to turn again and obey. Your faithfulness is awesome! Through Your Spirit, help me be faithful to You in return.

DAY 245

MORNING

IN THE MORNING

Let me hear Your loving-kindness in the morning, for I trust in You. Teach me the way I should go for I lift up my soul to You.

PSALM 143:8 NLV

Father God, I want to meet with You every morning. As I start out each day, give me ears to hear Your loving-kindness. Help me listen for Your Spirit all through my day. Then at night, whisper loving thoughts and make me ready to meet You again in the morning.

EVENING

ABUNDANTLY BLESSED

And God is able to bless you abundantly, so that in all things at all times, having all that you need, you will abound in every good work.

2 CORINTHIANS 9:8 NIV

Father God, You bless me far beyond anything I could imagine. You bless me so much that I'll never *not* have what I need to do the good works You've planned for me. Help me give and give, as Your faithful worker, because You give and give even more.

MORNING

GOD'S LOVING EYE

I will instruct you and teach you in the way you should go; I will counsel you with my loving eye on you.

PSALM 32:8 NIV

Lord, I've seen dogs who follow their master's gaze, looking where their master looks and knowing what their master wants them to do. Help me be like that with You. Keep me so tuned in to You that I can easily discern what You want me to do and where You want me to go.

EVENING

GOODNESS AND MERCY

Surely goodness and mercy shall follow me all the days of my life; and I will dwell in the house of the LORD forever.

PSALM 23:6 NKJV

Lord, Your goodness and mercy are with me *every* day of my life, not just the happy ones. I might feel sad and doubtful, but You're still good and merciful. Help me focus on the future that You've promised I'll spend with You in heaven. Thank You for Your goodness and mercy.

MORNING

A CAGED BIRD SINGING

Be happy that you are able to share some of the suffering of Christ. When His shining-greatness is shown, you will be filled with much joy.

1 PETER 4:13 NLV

Father God, thank You for Paul and Silas. They prayed and sang hymns from their jail cell while the other prisoners were listening. Nothing like that has ever happened to me, Lord, and I'm glad. But I pray that I'll be faithful to praise You in any difficult situation—because people are listening.

EVENING

GOD BESIDE ME

But you are near, O LORD, and all your commands are true.

PSALM 119:151 NLT

Thank You, Lord, for this double promise that You always stay near me and never change Your truths. Your faithfulness in all my troubles deserves my praise, Lord. No one stands by me like You. There's nothing You won't do for me as long as I'm faithful too. Help me walk closely with You, following Your commands all my days. Amen.

MORNING

MOVING AND MAKING FRIENDS

A man who has friends must himself be friendly.

PROVERBS 18:24 NKJV

Father God, I don't like change. I'd rather stay in my comfort zone, but here I am in a new environment. I miss my old friends so much. I feel like crying just thinking about them. But it's time to square my shoulders, walk in, smile, introduce myself, and meet some new people. I guess I can think of them as "pre"-friends. Help me not to chicken out!

EVENING

BEFORE BIRTH

You saw me before I was born. Every day of my life was recorded in your book. Every moment was laid out before a single day had passed.

PSALM 139:16 NLT

God, even before I was born, You knew just what every day of my life would be like. Wow! When my days seem out of control, I have to remind myself that I don't need to worry. Nothing in this life is beyond Your authority—and I can trust You!

MORNING

FOR MY GOOD

The Lord Who bought you and saves you, the Holy One of Israel, says, "I am the Lord your God, Who teaches you to do well, Who leads you in the way you should go."
ISAIAH 48:17 NLV

Sometimes I forget, Lord, that Your guidance is always for my good. Sometimes it feels like taking medicine. But I know You want what's best for me and that Your paths always lead to good things. Teach me to trust You more every day.

EVENING

ANGER

Get rid of all bitterness, rage and anger, brawling and slander, along with every form of malice.
EPHESIANS 4:31 NIV

Lord, I'm angry and frustrated, and I need Your help. I need to do something with these feelings, and so I choose to give them to You. Help me move past them. Bring peace to a situation that seems so out of control. Show me my part in this fight, and speak to the other girl's heart too. We *both* need Your healing. Amen.

MORNING

OPEN EARS

Your ears shall hear a word behind you, saying, "This is the way, walk in it," whenever you turn to the right hand or whenever you turn to the left.

ISAIAH 30:21 NKJV

Lord, I don't always hear Your direction. Tune my ears so I'll hear only You. Help me know when it's You I'm hearing and when it's my own feelings or some other voice trying to imitate You. I want to know exactly which way to go.

EVENING

JOY IS ON THE WAY

Weeping may last through the night, but joy comes with the morning.

PSALM 30:5 NLT

Lord, I've had a really bad day. I can't imagine being happy again, but You're telling me that my tears and sadness won't last forever. You're looking out for me. You're getting good things ready. I can't see them, but You can. And I could never tell You thank You enough for watching over my life, for making sure that joy is in my future.

DAY 251

MORNING

THE TRUTH

"Then you will know the truth,
and the truth will set you free."
JOHN 8:32 NIV

Heavenly Father, ever since the devil whispered in Eve's ear and she listened, we've all been falling for his lies. We're tricked into believing him about so many things. I need You every second, Lord, to help me sort through the chatter in my head, so I know what to listen to and what to ignore. I want to know the truth—*Your* truth. Amen.

EVENING

WHERE'S MY CONFIDENCE?

"But blessed is the one who trusts in
the LORD, whose confidence is in him."
JEREMIAH 17:7 NIV

I'm confident because of You, Lord. You're the one who controls everything. My situation looks small and simple to You, and nothing I deal with surprises You. Thank You for giving me this promise to hold on to when I'm feeling less than confident. Although I might not see it, You *are* blessing me. Help me keep trusting You.

MORNING

THE LORD'S DELIGHT

No, the LORD's delight is in those who fear him,
those who put their hope in his unfailing love.
PSALM 147:11 NLT

You delight in me, Lord. Sometimes I can't believe that You love me this way, but it's true! I want everything I do—*my whole life*—to honor You and make You happy. That should be easy, since You give me so many good reasons to obey You; but I know I'll still need Your help to be faithful. You won't fail me!

EVENING

RECONCILIATION

Be kind to each other, tenderhearted, forgiving one another, just as God through Christ has forgiven you.
EPHESIANS 4:32 NLT

Lord, my friend and I aren't talking. We had a fight, and now things are so awkward when we're around each other. This new distance between us feels really weird because we used to be best friends. I'm still hurt by what she said, but please help me do the right thing. What should I do tomorrow—or even right now—to start mending this friendship?

DAY 253

MORNING

NO MORE CROOKED PATHS

"I will bring the blind by a way they did not know; I will lead them in paths they have not known. I will make darkness light before them, and crooked places straight. These things I will do for them, and not forsake them."

ISAIAH 42:16 NKJV

Lord, life right now—it feels like I'm stumbling through a dark maze. But one day, when I look back, I'll see that You were making all these crooked paths run absolutely straight.

EVENING

THE CHANGELESS ONE

The LORD is gracious and full of compassion, slow to anger and great in mercy.

PSALM 145:8 NKJV

When I don't understand why certain things are happening, I often start questioning You, Lord. I start wondering if You're really good. Then You remind me that my circumstances might change majorly, but You never change. No matter how I'm feeling, You're still gracious, compassionate, forgiving, and merciful. Help me stop these doubts that are separating me from You. Amen.

MORNING

LITTLE MARY QUITE EXTRAORDINARY

"For He who is mighty has done great things for me, and holy is His name."

LUKE 1:49 NKJV

Father God, thank You for Mary, this girl who became the mother of Jesus. She found favor in Your eyes and became a witness to the Incarnation, the defining event of history. Lord, You love to turn our expectations on their heads! Help me be more like Mary, always open to what You want to do through me.

EVENING

GREATER UNDERSTANDING

Your hands made me and put me together. Give me understanding to learn Your Law.

PSALM 119:73 NLV

Lord God, the Bible is Your Word for my life. Help me understand what You're saying to me through it. Feed my spirit and fill me with Your wisdom as I read Your words, so I can grow and learn more about You. Bring the words I read back to my mind when I need them for whatever I'm facing.

DAY 255

MORNING

PATH OF LIFE

You will show me the path of life; in Your presence is fullness of joy; at Your right hand are pleasures forevermore.

PSALM 16:11 NKJV

Father God, sometimes my way seems better to me, so I take a side trip off Your path only to find that things don't go so well. I know that only Your path leads to life, to joy, to pleasures that last forever. So I'll put blinders on my eyes, Lord, and look straight ahead to You.

EVENING

FAITHFUL IN TRIALS

"Yahweh! The LORD! The God of compassion and mercy! I am slow to anger and filled with unfailing love and faithfulness."

EXODUS 34:6 NLT

Lord, when life is challenging, I'm tempted to think evil has won. It hasn't. This promise of who You are, so unfailing in love and faithfulness, holds true forever. Troubles might come, but I pray that You would keep me mindful of Your mercy even during my worst days. Help me see Your work in everything.

MORNING

WHEN FORGIVENESS IS HARD

"Forgive, and you will be forgiven."
LUKE 6:37 NIV

Lord, I'm struggling to forgive. Each time I invite You to come into a situation and help me forgive, it feels like the hardest thing I've ever done. I lay my burden at the cross and feel lighter. . . but then I walk over and pick it up again. I'm looking to You, Jesus. Help me follow You and forgive just as You forgive me.

EVENING

ENDURING LOVE

Give thanks to the God of gods.
His faithful love endures forever.
PSALM 136:2 NLT

Lord, nothing can stop Your love, because no one and nothing is greater than You. Thanksgiving fills my heart and my mouth as I rely on Your love. Keep me faithful through all my troubles. Help me hold on to Your love and draw near to You because no one else cares for me like You do. No one else brings me so much joy. Thank You, Lord, for Your love that goes on and on and on.

DAY 257

MORNING

STANDING UP STRAIGHT

Teach me to do Your will, for You are my God;
Your Spirit is good. Lead me in the land of uprightness.
PSALM 143:10 NKJV

My burdens have been feeling extra heavy lately, Father. Maybe You've noticed my shoulders slumped, my head hanging low. Remind me that I don't need to carry these burdens—that You're strong enough to carry all the weight of the world. I give You my worries. Help me stand upright and follow Your perfect way.

EVENING

GLADNESS

The humble will see their God at work and be glad.
Let all who seek God's help be encouraged.
PSALM 69:32 NLT

Father God, Your joy should be the theme for every one of my days. A lot of the time, trials squeeze gladness from my life. But my troubles don't have to rule over me. Thank You for the promise, Lord, that if I humbly draw closer to You, then I will see You in my life and be glad.

DAY 258

MORNING

MENTORS

Older women are to teach the young women to love their husbands and children.

TITUS 2:4 NLV

Dear Father God, the Bible says that older women should teach young women. I need a mentor in my life right now, one I can learn from, one who can teach me about You and how You want me to live. I ask You to send someone like that my way. And when I get older, enable me to be a mentor too. Amen.

EVENING

ETERNAL LIFE

"Just as Moses lifted up the snake in the wilderness, so the Son of Man must be lifted up, that everyone who believes may have eternal life in him."

JOHN 3:14–15 NIV

Your sacrifice, Jesus, made my new life possible. Because I believe in You, I know I'll never really die. Help me live each day aware of the price You paid. Give me confidence that You'll work out Your life in me every day, no matter what problems I face.

MORNING

SHOW AND LEAD

Point out anything in me that offends you,
and lead me along the path of everlasting life.
PSALM 139:24 NLT

You know, Lord God, how I try to hide sin inside my heart. But I can't hide it from You. Show me where I need to change and grow to be more like You. Bring into my life true godly friends who can help me where I struggle. And lead me in Your path that leads to forever life.

EVENING

PATIENCE, PATIENCE

Endings are better than beginnings.
Sticking to it is better than standing out.
ECCLESIASTES 7:8 MSG

Lord, I'll admit it: I'm not very patient. I start something new, but then the excitement wears off. And if things don't go the way I want them to, I feel like doing something else. But You never give up on what You've started. You never give up on me! Help me be more like You so I keep doing the right things until they're finished.

MORNING

PRAYING FOR ENEMIES

"But I tell you, love your enemies and pray for those who persecute you, that you may be children of your Father in heaven."
MATTHEW 5:44–45 NIV

Lord, thank You for this verse. I can't hold on to my negative feelings about a person if I'm praying for them. And when it feels impossible to love my enemies, Your words encourage me to obey. You empower me to obey! And Your Word shows me why I should.

EVENING

MY ROCK

But the LORD's plans stand firm forever; his intentions can never be shaken.
PSALM 33:11 NLT

It's hard to imagine plans that never change, Lord. But I'm glad You and Your purposes stay the same, because I need a Rock to stand on, a foundation that will never shift. I may not see Your design for my life, but that doesn't matter. You're still controlling the "out of control." You're still directing everything so it turns out perfectly. I can count on it!

DAY 261

MORNING

THE SAME OLD ME

You have searched me, LORD, and you know me.

PSALM 139:1 NIV

Lord, today I'm a little discouraged. I have a feeling I could do much more for You if my personality were different or if I didn't have any flaws. Help me to love myself like You do. Help me be the best *me* I can be. And even though I'll always be imperfect, use me anyway! Use me so that You get the glory.

EVENING

REST ASSURED

"Be still, and know that I am God; I will be exalted among the nations, I will be exalted in the earth."

PSALM 46:10 NIV

Lord, You are awesome! I'm learning that I can be at peace because You have a plan. You can handle anything—including my entire life. You are powerful, sovereign, and wise, and You never drop the ball. Because of who You are, I can be still. I can be confident no matter what. Thank You!

MORNING

FUTURE GLORY

I am sure that our suffering now cannot be compared to the shining-greatness that He is going to give us.

ROMANS 8:18 NLV

When it comes down to it, Father God, it's not all about me. I'm guilty of being so selfish, so self-centered, so "me focused" that I lose sight of the big picture. Lord, when pain surrounds me, let me see just a little bit of the shining-greatness that's coming. Help me live today with future glory in mind.

EVENING

PEACE WITH OTHERS

Live in peace with each other.

1 THESSALONIANS 5:13 NIV

Lord, I need Your peace. Some people are just hard to be around. They talk too much or do annoying things. Our personalities rub each other the wrong way. I need the Holy Spirit's power to stay calm. I don't want to get frustrated or lose my temper. Put Your loving ways in me so I can do everything I can to live in peace with everybody.

DAY 263

MORNING

AN ETERNAL GLORY

For our present troubles are small and won't last very long. Yet they produce for us a glory that vastly outweighs them and will last forever!
2 CORINTHIANS 4:17 NLT

When I think about eternity, Lord, I realize the time I spend on earth is pretty insignificant. But I still tend to get fixated on my daily problems and start to feel hopeless. Today, Lord, I'll let Your power get me through whatever happens. Use my troubles to transform me for eternity.

EVENING

FINDING CONTENTMENT

But godliness with contentment is great gain.
1 TIMOTHY 6:6 NIV

Lord, please help me find my contentment in You. I don't want to be defined by "stuff"—the things I own or the things I do. My greatest happiness is knowing who You are and who I am in Jesus. I gain so much more by being like You than by getting more and more stuff. Help me know real, soul-deep contentment as I spend time with You. Amen.

MORNING

STRENGTH TO FORGIVE

But you belong to God, my dear children. You have already won a victory over those people, because the Spirit who lives in you is greater than the spirit who lives in the world.

1 JOHN 4:4 NLT

Lord, thank You for not giving up on me as I learn to forgive. I remember the first time You helped me win this battle. I felt so good. And I was stronger. So, Lord, keep strengthening me for the harder battles to come.

EVENING

MANAGING MY AFFAIRS

She watches over the affairs of her household and does not eat the bread of idleness.

PROVERBS 31:27 NIV

Father God, I don't have a household to run like my mom does. But I still have certain things that are my responsibility. I know it's important to not be lazy; and the truth is, I feel a lot better when I get everything done instead of putting it off. Please help me with this, Lord—I need You!

DAY 265

MORNING

THE LORD'S PURPOSE

You can make many plans,
but the LORD's purpose will prevail.
PROVERBS 19:21 NLT

Lord, the future seems so unpredictable when I think about all that could happen. Right now, I put every one of my plans in Your hands. Take control of everything I do and say. Show me Your purpose in my life, or lead me in the right direction even when I don't understand Your plan. More than anything, I want Your goals to be my goals. Amen.

EVENING

WONDERFULLY MADE

I praise you because I am fearfully and wonderfully made.
PSALM 139:14 NIV

Father God, You know how I went clothes shopping with my friends this week? Well, it wasn't much fun because I ended up feeling pretty bad about myself. I tried on some things that look great on my friends, but they looked *awful* on me. When I start to believe that I'm not good enough, Lord, remind me that I'm wonderfully made—that there are all kinds of beautiful.

MORNING

GREAT HOPE

We are to be looking for the great hope and the coming of our great God and the One Who saves, Christ Jesus.
TITUS 2:13 NLV

Father God, whenever I'm disappointed, help me focus on You. When things seem hopeless, help me zero in on the hope that You give. The hope the Bible talks about is real. The hope I have in You, Lord, is for the future—but it blesses me today too. It's great hope from a great God!

EVENING

FAMILY PRAYERS

He and all his family were devout and God-fearing; he gave generously to those in need and prayed to God regularly.
ACTS 10:2 NIV

Lord, my family doesn't pray together very often. We say a quick prayer before we eat, but that's about it. I want to pray with my family, but I'm not sure how. Show me where to start, Lord. Maybe I could ask my mom to pray with me? Please make my family a family that prays.

DAY 267

MORNING

WHEN CHRIST APPEARS

When Christ who is our life appears,
then you also will appear with Him in glory.
COLOSSIANS 3:4 NKJV

Jesus, I look forward to Your return to earth. I'm so thankful that I'm not on my own—that You're with me all the way. Thank You for the gift of Your Holy Spirit who lives in me and helps me live for God. You're my life now, and You'll take me with You into heaven, where I'll be made perfect.

EVENING

SERVING THE LORD

"But if serving the LORD seems undesirable to you,
then choose for yourselves this day whom you will serve. . . .
But as for me and my household, we will serve the LORD."
JOSHUA 24:15 NIV

Lord, I could give my allegiance to so many different people or causes in this world. Please strengthen me to serve You. As I bow before You, I ask You to supply all that I need so I can go out and bless the people around me. Amen.

DAY 268

MORNING

THE POWER OF WORDS

The tongue can bring death or life; those who love to talk will reap the consequences.

PROVERBS 18:21 NLT

Heavenly Father, keep me aware of my words. Help me apologize if I've hurt anyone with something I've said. And more than that, help me think about what I'm going to say before I say it. My words are powerful. They can be positive or negative for someone else. Remind me to speak only positive things today.

EVENING

RENEWING MY MIND

Do not conform to the pattern of this world, but be transformed by the renewing of your mind. Then you will be able to test and approve what God's will is—his good, pleasing and perfect will.

ROMANS 12:2 NIV

Lord, sometimes my emotions need a makeover. I ask for Your power to change any negative patterns in my thinking. Help me renew my mind and express myself in ways that build others up. Help me know Your will in everything.

DAY 269

MORNING

GOD'S THOUGHTS

For I know the thoughts that I think toward you, says the LORD, thoughts of peace and not of evil, to give you a future and a hope.

JEREMIAH 29:11 NKJV

Father God, teach me to think Your thoughts: thoughts of peace and goodness that will lead me into the future You have planned for me. Show me the steps I should take to enjoy the abundant life You want me to live, both here on earth and in heaven.

EVENING

TRANSFORMING MY THOUGHTS

May the words of my mouth and the meditation of my heart be pleasing to you, O LORD, my rock and my redeemer.

PSALM 19:14 NLT

Father God, the Bible says I can choose what to think about. Transform my thoughts with the wisdom and insight found in scripture. When I read the Bible, help me remember Your words. Then when my mind wanders to something that doesn't make You happy, I'll think about what You've said instead of the other stuff.

DAY 270

MORNING

A PEBBLE

"You did not choose me, but I chose you and appointed you so that you might go and bear fruit—fruit that will last."

JOHN 15:16 NIV

Sometimes I feel like I don't make a difference, Lord. Like I'll never be able to help people or change the world. Thank You for reminding me what You think. You've planned for me to bear fruit. I'm only one tiny pebble thrown into the sea, but my ripples travel! Amen.

EVENING

RESCUE

The LORD says, "I will rescue those who love me. I will protect those who trust in my name."

PSALM 91:14 NLT

You will rescue the people who love You, Jesus. What a great promise! So many times You've sent me help before I could even ask, and I'm so thankful for Your provision. Now I need Your rescue again, Lord. My situation might not change, but You can make a change in me. Work in my life, please. Rescue me!

MORNING

BEFORE THE WORLD BEGAN

This truth also gives hope of life that lasts forever. God promised this before the world began. He cannot lie.

TITUS 1:2 NLV

You never lie, Lord God—You *can't* lie! Your promises are better than gold. They reach forward into eternity—and they reach backward, before the earth was formed. There is no place in the history of everything where You're not present, so why should I worry about my life right now? Hold me in Your hand today.

EVENING

PRAISING WHEN I'M HURTING

Great is the LORD! He is most worthy of praise! No one can measure his greatness.

PSALM 145:3 NLT

Lord, I'm hurting right now; You know all about it. But I choose to praise You anyway. You are great, and no one else is worthy of the honor and glory due You. I give You my problems and trust You to turn them into possibilities. Let my heart long only for Your comfort and time spent with You.

MORNING

GOD'S RICHES

Oh, how great are God's riches and wisdom and knowledge! How impossible it is for us to understand his decisions and his ways!

ROMANS 11:33 NLT

When I start to worry about my life, Lord—when I start to feel like You might not know what You're doing—remind me that Your riches are much greater than my needs. Give me a spirit of peace when I don't understand the *whys*. You *are* doing good things in my life.

EVENING

THE FRUIT OF THE SPIRIT

But the fruit that comes from having the Holy Spirit in our lives is: love, joy, peace, not giving up, being kind, being good, having faith, being gentle, and being the boss over our own desires.

GALATIANS 5:22–23 NLV

Lord, I see some of the fruit of the Spirit in my life. But I definitely could use Your help to develop these fruits and produce more. Please work within me to cultivate good-quality fruit, Lord. I want to be everything that's in these verses.

MORNING

THE MISSING LINK

And God said, "Let there be light," and there was light. God saw that the light was good, and he separated the light from the darkness.

GENESIS 1:3–4 NIV

Father God, some people try to explain life without including You, but there's no way this world could've been created without You—the Creator. It's way too complex to have just happened. You're such an awesome God! Thank You for Your amazing love that gives us life and keeps the world spinning.

EVENING

NEW FRIENDS

If one person falls, the other can reach out and help. But someone who falls alone is in real trouble.

ECCLESIASTES 4:10 NLT

Lord, some people are just plain hard to love. Help me look beyond their annoying qualities to the special person You created. You love every one of us and want us to love each other. No one deserves to be alone, Lord. Give me the courage to reach out to people and make new friends.

MORNING

ALL GRACE

And the God of all grace, who called you to his eternal glory in Christ, after you have suffered a little while, will himself restore you and make you strong, firm and steadfast.

1 PETER 5:10 NIV

Father God, Your grace is so powerful that it can work through the toughest times. Please comfort me in my times of suffering, and remind me that in the end, I can count on You to make me perfect and strong.

EVENING

GIVING GOD CONTROL

We can make our plans, but the LORD determines our steps.

PROVERBS 16:9 NLT

Jesus, You knew that Your Father's will was for You to give Your life so we could have a relationship with You. You gave up control. Help me do that too. I was created for a specific purpose. You have a plan for my life, and I want to finish everything I was created to do. Help me live my life following Your plan.

MORNING

ENDLESS POWER

God is able to do much more than we ask or think through His power working in us.
EPHESIANS 3:20 NLV

Father God, too often I put limits on what is possible in my life. But nothing is impossible for You. Help me remember the miracles You've done. Give me a heart to believe You can do much more than anything I ask or think, and give me Your eyes to see the endless power that's working in me.

EVENING

GUARDED PATHS

He guards the paths of the just and protects those who are faithful to him.
PROVERBS 2:8 NLT

Lord, I can count on Your promise to protect me. It doesn't always seem like I can when I'm in the middle of a problem. Help me trust in You anyway. Keep me faithful to You no matter what I'm going through. And thank You for bringing good out of my troubles, Lord. I will trust in You for *all* things.

MORNING

OBSIDIAN

"The LORD lives! Blessed be my Rock!
Let God be exalted, the Rock of my salvation!"
2 SAMUEL 22:47 NKJV

Lord, sometimes I struggle to keep trusting You. The Bible calls You the Rock, but sometimes I think You're more like lava. I walk gingerly because I don't trust that I have a firm footing. But You have proven to be faithful to me in the past. You have *always* been a solid rock beneath me. Please make my faith as solid.

EVENING

A BROKEN FRIENDSHIP

Above all, love each other deeply,
because love covers over a multitude of sins.
1 PETER 4:8 NIV

Lord, my friend has hurt me. She has done something that isn't easy to forgive. But. . .if I'm being honest, I've probably done some things that have hurt her too. You've loved me so much—even when I've sinned. Your love mends my brokenness. Help me love my friend like that. Thank You for being with me as we put this friendship back together.

DAY 277

MORNING

A SPIRIT OF POWER

For God has not given us a spirit of fear,
but of power and of love and of a sound mind.
2 TIMOTHY 1:7 NKJV

Father God, I have this thing I'm really afraid of. I ask You to help me. I don't want my phobia to keep me from living the life You have planned for me. And You don't want me to be fearful either. Show me that You're in control whenever I'm afraid.

EVENING

A PENNY SAVED

The wise store up choice food and
olive oil, but fools gulp theirs down.
PROVERBS 21:20 NIV

Lord, my parents want me to save part of my allowance every week, but honestly, I don't see the point. I'll have plenty of time to save money when I'm older and have a job. Help me understand why it's good to save a little instead of spending it all. Help me see money like You do so I'll be smart about it.

MORNING

SHINING MORE AND MORE

The path of the righteous is like the morning sun,
shining ever brighter till the full light of day.
PROVERBS 4:18 NIV

Lord, the closer I am to You, the clearer Your will is to me. Thank You for the light that shines brighter with each step I take. When the light seems dim or I'm not sure which way to go, pull me close and lead me. Thank You for never giving up on me.

EVENING

A RIGHT PERSPECTIVE

We are the temple of the living God. As God has said:
"I will live with them and walk among them, and I
will be their God, and they will be my people."
2 CORINTHIANS 6:16 NIV

Father God, sometimes I wish I looked different. Remind me that I'm special because You made me! You chose me to be Your temple on earth. I want to take care of this body You've given me. My body belongs to You, Lord! Amen.

DAY 279

MORNING

PACK NOTHING BUT FAITH

Now faith is being sure we will get what we hope for. It is being sure of what we cannot see.

HEBREWS 11:1 NLV

Father God, Your world is so beautiful and *big*. I have a long list of all the places I want to see someday. But even if I never see them, I know I can count on seeing even more beautiful places in eternity. I praise You for what is and what will be.

EVENING

WHO I AM

For God wanted them to know that the riches and glory of Christ are for you Gentiles, too. And this is the secret: Christ lives in you. This gives you assurance of sharing his glory.

COLOSSIANS 1:27 NLT

Jesus, help me find my identity in You. As I read the Bible, give me an understanding of who You created me to be. Point out the true identity that is mine through salvation and my relationship with You.

MORNING

FIXING MY THOUGHTS

Fix your thoughts on what is true, and honorable, and right, and pure, and lovely, and admirable.
PHILIPPIANS 4:8 NLT

Father God, I've been having a pity party today. My thoughts are so focused on earthly things that I'm having trouble looking up. Lord, I know You can't work through me when I'm feeling sorry for myself. Forgive me for my pettiness, and help me live with more maturity. Direct my thoughts to good, praiseworthy things. In Jesus' name. Amen.

EVENING

HOPE IN GOD

Why are you sad, O my soul? Why have you become troubled within me? Hope in God, for I will praise Him again for His help of being near me.
PSALM 42:5 NLV

Lord, do You see my tears? Help me remember that even when I'm down, I can hope in You. Instead of telling myself lies that make me sadder, I can look to Your truth. Remind me of the good things You've done and Your promise to be near me now.

DAY 281

MORNING

LIKE JESUS

Dear friends, now we are children of God, and what we will be has not yet been made known. But we know that when Christ appears, we shall be like him, for we shall see him as he is.

1 JOHN 3:2 NIV

Lord Jesus, You're not done with me yet. I won't be finished until You come again to earth and take me home with You. I'm looking forward to that day, Lord—the day I will finally be like Jesus.

EVENING

GOD'S SHELTERING PRESENCE

The LORD is a shelter for the oppressed,
a refuge in times of trouble.

PSALM 9:9 NLT

Lord, when hurts go deep, I need a place where I'll be understood and loved. Thank You for sheltering me. Thank You for being a refuge when problems seem to suck all the joy out of me. It's like Your arms are wrapped around me every second! And because Your Spirit lives in me, You'll always be right here, guarding my heart.

MORNING

FACE-TO-FACE

Now that which we see is as if we were looking in a broken mirror. But then we will see everything. Now I know only a part. But then I will know everything in a perfect way. That is how God knows me right now.

1 CORINTHIANS 13:12 NLV

Lord, You know I can't see You clearly yet. I'm happy, though, that I will see You face-to-face someday, and then I'll finally truly know You—just like You know me perfectly right now.

EVENING

CHRIST CAN SAVE

Therefore he is able, once and forever, to save those who come to God through him. He lives forever to intercede with God on their behalf.

HEBREWS 7:25 NLT

Lord, a lot of bad people are in this world; but no matter how bad they seem to me, You can still save them. Help me share who You are with everybody I meet. Help me show them that You won't let anybody be lost if they believe in You and receive You as Savior.

DAY 283

MORNING

UNFADING BEAUTY

Clothe yourselves instead with the beauty that comes from within, the unfading beauty of a gentle and quiet spirit, which is so precious to God.

1 PETER 3:4 NLT

Father God, it's crazy to think that one day I'll be old and wrinkly, but I know that no one is young forever. Help me so I don't become obsessed with how I look. If I'm focused on spiritual things, I'll have a kind of beauty that will never fade.

EVENING

GOD'S CHILD

Everyone who believes that Jesus is the Christ has become a child of God.

1 JOHN 5:1 NLT

Father God, I'm Your daughter. Forgive me for the times I haven't lived up to that name. I want to be so full of Your personality that others see You in me. I never want anything I say or do to reflect negatively on You. I want to be like Jesus, because people could easily see that He was Yours.

MORNING

GLORY TO GLORY

But we all, with unveiled face, beholding as in a mirror the glory of the Lord, are being transformed into the same image from glory to glory, just as by the Spirit of the Lord.

2 CORINTHIANS 3:18 NKJV

Lord, You are glorious! And You share Your glory with me. You've created my very essence so it shines. And as I lock my eyes on You, You make me even shinier. Keep transforming me to look like You, Lord. Amen.

EVENING

A SURE THING

Those who have been ransomed by the LORD will return. They will enter Jerusalem singing, crowned with everlasting joy. Sorrow and mourning will disappear, and they will be filled with joy and gladness.

ISAIAH 51:11 NLT

Father God, I haven't seen an overwhelming amount of sadness in my life, but I know how horrible it is. Thank You for Your promise that sorrow will become singing, that grief will become gladness. One day we will live with You for eternity. You will make everything okay.

MORNING

BRAND NEW

He who was seated on the throne said,
"I am making everything new!"
REVELATION 21:5 NIV

Lord, this might sound silly, but today I feel like one of my old pairs of jeans with stains on them and holes in the knees. I wonder if You can do anything with my life because of all the mistakes I've made. So I'm choosing to believe what the Bible says. You're mending my flaws. You're redeeming me. You're making everything new!

EVENING

FAITHFUL PROMISES

Every word of God is pure; He is a shield
to those who put their trust in Him.
PROVERBS 30:5 NKJV

You don't make promises You won't keep, Lord. Your Word is 100 percent true. So when You say You'll be my shield because I've trusted in You, I can believe it. You'll give me all the help I need whenever I'm in trouble. You'll stay next to me no matter what happens. You promise!

MORNING

STRENGTH TO STRENGTH

They go from strength to strength.
PSALM 84:7 KJV

You know the strength I'll need for today, Lord. You know the strength I'll need for tomorrow, for next week, for next year. You know the strength I'll need for every one of the hard things that is in my future. Thank You that I don't have to worry about anything. You'll lead me from strength to strength, like jumping from stone to stone across a river. You'll always make me strong.

EVENING

DEAL WITH ANGER

"In your anger do not sin": Do not let the sun go down while you are still angry.
EPHESIANS 4:26 NIV

Lord, I need Your help. Sometimes I get *sooo* mad! I want to handle my anger in healthy ways. Help me process how I'm feeling and not just ignore it. Help me control my temper and talk about what bothers me while staying calm. Show me how to give my anger to You so I can be at peace!

MORNING

CALM MY HEART

For God has not given us a spirit of fear and timidity, but of power, love, and self-discipline.
2 TIMOTHY 1:7 NLT

Lord, calm my racing heart, please. Fill me with Your strength and courage. My problems feel like they're going to overcome me, but You've overcome the world and won't let me be brought down. You've given me a spirit of power, love, and self-discipline—not of fear. I feel braver already just remembering this awesome truth! Thank You, Lord.

EVENING

WHAT WILL BE

"For the earth shall be full of the knowledge of the LORD as the waters cover the sea."
ISAIAH 11:9 NKJV

Father God, the more I learn about Your creation, the more I'm amazed by You. The world is so complex and beautiful, and we're only just beginning to understand all its mysteries. Thank You for letting us get to know You—the one who created everything. Thank You that one day Your creation will be brimming with the knowledge of You.

MORNING

NO COVETING

Let your conduct be without covetousness.
HEBREWS 13:5 NKJV

Father God, it's so easy to break the tenth commandment: Do not covet. So many people are always looking at their lives and wanting what other people have. But You say we shouldn't compare ourselves with other people or envy them and what they have. Whatever You've given me I should enjoy, not hold up for inspection. Teach me to be truly thankful for Your blessings. In Jesus' name. Amen.

EVENING

TAKING UP MY CROSS

Then he said to the crowd, "If any of you wants to be my follower, you must give up your own way, take up your cross daily, and follow me."
LUKE 9:23 NLT

You've given me eternal life, Jesus. There's nothing I can do that will make me more or less saved, but I want to live for You. I'm not sure I completely understand what it means to take up my cross, but I pray that You would show me.

MORNING

WITH JESUS

"Father, I want those you have given me to be with me where I am, and to see my glory, the glory you have given me because you loved me before the creation of the world."

JOHN 17:24 NIV

Sometimes I wish I knew what's in my future, Jesus, but only You know what will happen. Instead of worrying, I want to just follow You into tomorrow. I don't really care where You lead me—as long as You're there too.

EVENING

THE GOSPEL FOR KIDS

You have known the Holy Writings since you were a child. They are able to give you wisdom that leads to being saved from the punishment of sin by putting your trust in Christ Jesus.

2 TIMOTHY 3:15 NLV

Heavenly Father, I learned about You and believed in Jesus when I was just a little kid. Now that I'm older, help me tell younger kids about You. Some people might think kids can't understand, but You make Your message clear.

MORNING

JOY

"You will go out in joy and be led forth in peace;
the mountains and hills will burst into song before you,
and all the trees of the field will clap their hands."
ISAIAH 55:12 NIV

Lord, some days things go so well that all creation seems to be singing to You, and I join in. Other days, I don't feel like praising. Thank You for the reminder that no matter what happens today, You promise me joy.

EVENING

SLOW DOWN

Careful planning puts you ahead in the long run;
hurry and scurry puts you further behind.
PROVERBS 21:5 MSG

Lord, I know that being patient has benefits, but most of the time, I'm moving fast. I don't want to miss anything! Help me slow down. Help me take each thing as it comes. And help me appreciate interruptions, realizing that Your stops along the way are designed to let me experience Your best plans for my life.

DAY 291

MORNING

A MOUNTAIN VIEW

Let the rivers clap their hands, let the mountains sing together for joy.
PSALM 98:8 NIV

Father God, I praise You for mountains and the way they make me look up. So much of the time I'm focused on the pebbles on the ground—the little problems that trip me up and annoy me. Give me Your eyes, Lord. Help me see things up high like You do. And let me sing with the mountains about how awesome You are!

EVENING

JUST CRY OUT

For he will deliver the needy who cry out, the afflicted who have no one to help.
PSALM 72:12 NIV

Lord, You don't just stand beside me when I'm in trouble. You promise to deliver me. You give me everything I need and help me through anything. Please keep me connected to You so I'll share every single one of my problems with You. All I have to do is cry out to know You're taking care of me.

MORNING

LET IT BE

Then Mary said, "Behold the maidservant of the Lord! Let it be to me according to your word."

LUKE 1:38 NKJV

Lord, help me follow Mary's example when my world is rocked. She found out she was going to be Jesus' mother, and she wasn't even married. People probably didn't understand and criticized her. But she surrendered her life to You. I want to accept Your Word, no matter what it says to me, and surrender my life to You too.

EVENING

HIS AWESOME POWER

Say to God, "How awesome are your deeds! So great is your power. . . . All the earth bows down to you; they sing praise to you, they sing the praises of your name."

PSALM 66:3–4 NIV

Lord, You parted the Red Sea. You tell the wind and waves what to do. You raise people from the dead. Your power is awesome! Nothing is impossible for You. I bow before You now, singing praises to You.

DAY 293

MORNING

RIGHT MOTIVES

If you do ask, you do not receive because your reasons for asking are wrong. You want these things only to please yourselves.

JAMES 4:3 NLV

Father God, I admit that sometimes I'm guilty of treating You like a vending machine—if I say the right words in the right order, I'll get what I want. Today I ask that You would show me when my prayers are selfish. Give me pure motives, a clean heart, and a clear conscience.

EVENING

A LEARNING EXPERIENCE

We can rejoice, too, when we run into problems and trials, for we know that they help us develop endurance. And endurance develops strength of character, and character strengthens our confident hope of salvation.

ROMANS 5:3–4 NLT

Lord, thank You for Your patience as I learn from the problems I have and the hard things I go through. I can see how You're teaching me to keep going, how You're molding who I am. And that brings me joy!

MORNING

PRECIOUS ENCOURAGEMENT

A word spoken at the right time
is like fruit of gold set in silver.
PROVERBS 25:11 NLV

Father God, today I need encouraging words. You know that words are important to me. The other people in my world don't always realize the power of their words, but I know I can't expect other people to meet every need in my life. So, Lord, let me look to You and Your Word to find the encouragement I need. In Jesus' name. Amen.

EVENING

THE COMFORT OF THE SCRIPTURES

For whatever things were written before were written
for our learning, that we through the patience and
comfort of the Scriptures might have hope.
ROMANS 15:4 NKJV

Lord, our twisted, sinful natures have caused a lot of fear and sadness. But You've given me a way to be comforted. You've provided Your Word so that I can learn about You. I don't have to be defeated by this world. I have Your Word, and because of that I have hope.

MORNING

SHARING GOD'S WORDS

"But everything I said through my servants the prophets happened to your ancestors, just as I said. As a result, they repented."

ZECHARIAH 1:6 NLT

Father God, when I think about sharing the gospel, I think I need to have the perfect words planned out so I'll know exactly what to say. But the truth is, it's Your words that change people. You save sinners like me. Lord, from now on, I'll trust Your Word and its power to do what I can't.

EVENING

HELPED

The Lord helps them and takes them out of trouble. He takes them away from the sinful, and saves them, because they go to Him for a safe place.

PSALM 37:40 NLV

Lord, even in the middle of trouble, You've pulled me through. Even the biggest problems have worked themselves out. I know it's not because of any great thing I've done but rather because You've been smoothing the way for me. You are so great, Lord! Thank You for all the help You've given.

MORNING

CONFIDENCE

This is the confidence we have in approaching God: that if we ask anything according to his will, he hears us.

1 John 5:14 NIV

When I pray, Lord, I can be confident that You're listening and that You understand the thoughts behind my prayers even when I don't. I'm never talking into empty air! Help me ask for things that line up with Your will so I'll be confident that I'll get what I've asked for. Amen.

EVENING

TAKE IT TO HEART

Blessed is the one who reads aloud the words of this prophecy, and blessed are those who hear it and take to heart what is written in it, because the time is near.

Revelation 1:3 NIV

Father God, I know that what I do for You counts more than anything else. Guide me as I read the Bible so that I'll follow everything in it. Some parts are hard to understand, but You've promised to bless me for hearing and obeying.

MORNING

THE WAY

Jesus said to him, "I am the way, the truth, and the life. No one comes to the Father except through Me."

JOHN 14:6 NKJV

Jesus, You are the way, the truth, and the life. You show me how to draw near to God the Father so I can live an abundant life—the one You've planned for me. Help me not to be distracted by false paths that seem easier. Make my life an example for others so they'll want to follow You too.

EVENING

TIDINGS OF GREAT JOY

Then the angel said to them, "Do not be afraid, for behold, I bring you good tidings of great joy which will be to all people."

LUKE 2:10 NKJV

Father God, when I have good news, I can't wait to share it with everyone around me. But the best things that happen to me can't compare with the news the angels proclaimed on the night Jesus was born. Jesus is joy—the greatest joy ever. Help me keep sharing the news!

MORNING

A JOYFUL NOISE

Shout to the LORD, all the earth;
break out in praise and sing for joy!
PSALM 98:4 NLT

Father God, thank You for music. For singing and instruments. For birds and breezes and brooks! All Your creation should be singing praises to You all the time, every second of every day, with each breath we take. You are awesome, and You give us joy. Thank You for letting me join in and sing to You.

EVENING

JOY IN GOD'S WORD

"These things I have spoken to you, that My joy
may remain in you, and that your joy may be full."
JOHN 15:11 NKJV

Father God, You're my teacher and guide, and everything You've said in the Bible is for my benefit. You want me to have joy—overflowing joy—and for that joy to stick with me all my life. How glad I am to have a personal God who cares about me so much!

DAY 299

MORNING

UNITED

"Again, truly I tell you that if two of you on earth agree about anything they ask for, it will be done for them by my Father in heaven."

MATTHEW 18:19 NIV

Lord, thank You for the privilege of praying and worshipping with other Christians. Thank You that when we pray together You hear us; and when we gather together You're there with us. Help us be the living, breathing, active body of Christ we're meant to be.

EVENING

HEAVEN'S WISDOM

But the wisdom that comes from heaven is first of all pure. Then it gives peace. It is gentle and willing to obey. It is full of loving-kindness and of doing good. It has no doubts and does not pretend to be something it is not.

JAMES 3:17 NLV

Thank You, Lord, that Your wisdom is all good. Help me be wise like You when I make choices—because when I make wise choices, the goodness spreads to people around me too.

MORNING

AS SIMPLE AS THAT

"I believed in God, so I spoke."
2 CORINTHIANS 4:13 NLT

Lord, sometimes when people ask me about my faith, I can't seem to say anything. I'm so worried about saying the wrong thing. Or I'm worried they won't like me anymore or they'll think I'm dumb. Remind me in those times that sharing You with other people isn't complicated. I just have to say what I believe—and You'll be right there with me as I do.

EVENING

REFUGE AND STRENGTH

God is our refuge and strength,
a very present help in trouble.
PSALM 46:1 NKJV

If I need a safe place to hide from the world, You're there, Lord. But I know You don't let me avoid reality for long. Instead, You help me. With You by my side, I won't hide from life. Your help means I can live the way I'm supposed to live—focused on You. Help me rely on Your strength in every challenge.

DAY 301

MORNING

ABIDING

"If you abide in Me, and My words abide in you, you will ask what you desire, and it shall be done for you."

JOHN 15:7 NKJV

Lord, I want to abide in You as I pray. Keep my thoughts focused on You as I wait for You to respond. Give me peace and confidence to believe You'll work everything out for good. Then keep me close. Let me remain in You as I watch for the way You'll answer my prayers. Amen.

EVENING

BLESSED WITH FRIENDS

Perfume and incense bring joy to the heart, and the pleasantness of a friend springs from their heartfelt advice.

PROVERBS 27:9 NIV

Sometimes I feel so down, Lord, and then a friend blesses me through something they say or do, and I think of You. The love You give is what makes us want to reach out to others. Thank You for blessing my life with friends. Help me bless them too.

DAY 302

MORNING

A WAVERING HEART

But when you ask, you must believe and not doubt, because the one who doubts is like a wave of the sea, blown and tossed by the wind.

JAMES 1:6 NIV

You know how easily my heart wavers, Lord. I'm like a boat out in the ocean. I think I trust You, but then I begin to doubt. Help me have absolute faith so I'm not thrown around by every problem I have and every trouble I go through. Lord, take control!

EVENING

FOR THOSE WHO MOURN

"Blessed are those who mourn, for they will be comforted."

MATTHEW 5:4 NIV

Lord, my friend has a deep pain inside. Please comfort her. Be near to her, Lord. Help her rest in the loving arms of the one who loves her most. Heal her heartache. You know grief, so You know her pain. Help her know that You can relate and that You care. I pray she'll be able to smile again soon.

DAY 303

MORNING

STAYING TRUE

We think of those who stayed true to Him as happy even though they suffered. You have heard how long Job waited. You have seen what the Lord did for him in the end. The Lord is full of loving-kindness and pity.

JAMES 5:11 NLV

Lord, no matter what I'm going through, if I hold on to You, Your compassion and mercy always find me out. When I put my faith in Your promises, You always come through.

EVENING

LAUGHTER

We were filled with laughter, and we sang for joy. And the other nations said, "What amazing things the LORD has done."

PSALM 126:2 NLT

Father God, tonight I laughed until my sides ached, and it was *good*. Thank You for being a God whose miracles bring laughter—like with Sarah when her son was born and with the disciples and their huge catch of fish. You long to surprise us with joy!

MORNING

ANYTHING!

"Truly I tell you, if anyone says to this mountain, 'Go, throw yourself into the sea,' and does not doubt in their heart but believes that what they say will happen, it will be done for them."

MARK 11:23 NIV

I don't want to throw any mountains into the ocean, Lord—and I don't think that's the real meaning of Jesus' words here. Please show me the truth of this verse. Teach me to pray according to Your will.

EVENING

JESUS, OUR CONFIDENCE

In [Jesus] and through faith in him we may approach God with freedom and confidence.

EPHESIANS 3:12 NIV

Jesus, without You, I wouldn't have any real reason to be confident. But because of You. . .wow! I can have a relationship with God Almighty. I can walk right up to the Father in prayer without worrying that He doesn't want to hear from me. And what the world might think is impossible? I can do that too—through You!

DAY 305

MORNING

POWERFUL PRAYERS

The earnest prayer of a righteous person has great power and produces wonderful results.

JAMES 5:16 NLT

Lord, sometimes when I'm dealing with a problem, I forget to pray. I do everything I can to make things right, and then I remember that I should be praying for Your help. Prayer isn't just talking. It's powerful, because You're the one who answers prayers. Help me unleash that power in my world by praying about everything first.

EVENING

FULL REDEMPTION

Israel, put your hope in the LORD, for with the LORD is unfailing love and with him is full redemption.

PSALM 130:7 NIV

Lord, thank You for Your unfailing love. Your saving work didn't touch me for just one second; it reclaimed *every* second of my life. Whatever troubles I go through, You stay beside me, working out Your total redemption. Hope isn't just for heaven. It's for every day. Help me faithfully put my hope in You.

MORNING

GOOD COURAGE

Be of good courage, and He shall strengthen your heart, all you who hope in the LORD.

PSALM 31:24 NKJV

Where can I find strength when I feel like giving up? Only in You, Lord God. I lift my face to You and get the energy to keep going, like a flower soaking up the sun. Your Spirit leads me in the right direction. Your courage fills my heart. And that's all I need. Help me be of good courage always!

EVENING

WELL BEGUN IS HALF DONE

Now faith is the substance of things hoped for, the evidence of things not seen.

HEBREWS 11:1 NKJV

Father God, there's something You've asked me to do that I've been putting off. You keep reminding me to obey. Tonight I was suddenly happy, thinking that by tomorrow night I'll have started. This wasn't wishful thinking, was it, Lord? It was *faith*. Thank You for believing in what isn't visible in me yet and allowing me to do the same.

DAY 307

MORNING

LESSONS IN TRUST

I have put my trust in the Lord GOD,
that I may declare all Your works.
PSALM 73:28 NKJV

Heavenly Father, even though I know Your character and Your track record, I struggle to let You take control of some areas of my life. I say that I will. I try to rely on You. But I still find it hard to let You handle everything. Please take my hand and teach me to trust.

EVENING

NO MORE SORROW

"So with you: Now is your time of grief,
but I will see you again and you will rejoice,
and no one will take away your joy."
JOHN 16:22 NIV

Jesus, You told Your disciples that You were going away but would see them again. Those men had walked and talked with You. They must have felt lost. But three days later, when You rose from the grave. . .wow! You turned their grief into joy, and You do the same for us today. Thank You, Jesus!

MORNING

IN ALL MY WAYS

In all your ways submit to him,
and he will make your paths straight.
PROVERBS 3:6 NIV

Father God, help me give You every part of me, everything I do. Help me look only to You for direction so You'll make the path ahead of me straight. Teach me to trust You with all my heart and to not depend on my own understanding. You know everything that is best for me, and I submit to You!

EVENING

TRUTH IN SCRIPTURE

"You have shown me the ways of life.
I will be full of joy when I see Your face."
ACTS 2:28 NLV

Father God, in the Bible You show me the ways of life—I find out how to live by reading Your words. You reveal the truth to me, Lord, and nothing is greater than knowing what's true, because the truth leads me to You. I can only imagine the joy I'll feel when I see You face-to-face in heaven!

DAY 309

MORNING

A WILLING MIND

"Acknowledge the God of your father, and serve him with wholehearted devotion and with a willing mind, for the LORD searches every heart and understands every desire and every thought. If you seek him, he will be found by you."

1 CHRONICLES 28:9 NIV

Make my mind willing, Lord. Help me trust that Your plans for me are better than my own. Help me agree with Your ways for my life. I seek You—the one who understands me completely.

EVENING

WORKING WITH ALL MY HEART

Whatever you do, work at it with all your heart, as working for the Lord, not for human masters, since you know that you will receive an inheritance from the Lord as a reward. It is the Lord Christ you are serving.

COLOSSIANS 3:23–24 NIV

Father God, You know my attitude isn't always great. Sometimes I grumble when I have work to do. Help me see You as my boss. Help me do my best. Amen.

MORNING

THE GIVER

You open your hand and satisfy
the desires of every living thing.
PSALM 145:16 NIV

Lord, You've always given me the things I need. You even give me things that I don't "need" but are just fun. You've been taking care of me my whole life. I've never been on my own, Lord; and even when I grow up and I'm responsible for myself, You'll still be there. *Everything* comes from You. I praise You, my open-handed God!

EVENING

SWEET DREAMS

In peace I will lie down and sleep,
for you alone, O LORD, will keep me safe.
PSALM 4:8 NLT

Lord, I love to sleep! And because You're taking care of me—watching over me and keeping me safe even when I'm not awake—I can sleep without any worries. When thoughts keep me up, Lord, help me calm my brain so I can sleep peacefully again. When I'm connected to You, I have nothing to fear—ever!

DAY 311

MORNING

A LOYAL HEART

"So let your whole heart be true to the Lord our God. Walk in His Laws and keep His Word, just as you are doing today."
1 KINGS 8:61 NLV

Lord, I surrender my heart to You absolutely. Keep my heart and mind from wandering. I know I won't follow You perfectly, but You give me grace. Thank You for never abandoning me. Through this prayer, I commit myself totally to You and Your plan for my life.

EVENING

GOD'S HOLY NATION

For the holy nation of God is not food and drink. It is being right with God. It is peace and joy given by the Holy Spirit. If you follow Christ in these things, God will be happy with you.
ROMANS 14:17–18 NLV

Father God, Your kingdom isn't made of material things. What we eat and drink doesn't save us. Teach me what's important. Help me focus on being right with You and serving You so You'll be pleased with me. Amen.

MORNING

DIVINE GUIDANCE

If any of you lacks wisdom, you should ask God, who gives generously to all without finding fault, and it will be given to you.

JAMES 1:5 NIV

Father God, what is Your will? How can I know exactly what You want me to do? I ask today that You'd give me wisdom. Guide me as I figure out Your will. Your Word promises that You won't hold back, and You won't find fault with me when I ask for wisdom.

EVENING

A GIVING HEART

Remember the words of the Lord Jesus, how he said, It is more blessed to give than to receive.

ACTS 20:35 KJV

Lord, sometimes I don't feel like serving or giving to the church. My church is always asking for volunteers and encouraging us to tithe. Can't I just focus on me? I have my own stuff going on! But . . .I know You call me to put others before myself and promise to bless me when I do. Change my heart, Lord. Make me a giver.

DAY 313

MORNING

CELEBRATION

They celebrate your abundant goodness
and joyfully sing of your righteousness.
PSALM 145:7 NIV

Father God, so many people who don't know You see You as a kill-joy who stops them from doing fun things. But I know You better! You delight in saying yes to us. More important, You delight in us and want what's for our good forever—not just what's fun for a few minutes. And You're planning the ultimate party—one that will never end. I can't wait to join the celebration!

EVENING

JOYFUL IN HOPE

But joyful are those who have the God of Israel as
their helper, whose hope is in the LORD their God.
PSALM 146:5 NLT

Father God, I'm realizing that hope and joy go hand in hand. I'll have joy as long as I hope in You. I never have to face any day with hopelessness. No matter what happens, I can find joy because my hope isn't in my circumstances or this world. My hope is in You!

MORNING

A WILLING HEART

"I know also, my God, that You test the heart and have pleasure in uprightness. As for me, in the uprightness of my heart I have willingly offered all these things."
1 CHRONICLES 29:17 NKJV

Father God, I give You everything I have to offer, willingly and gladly. Please give me a whole heart to follow You and obey Your commandments. Keep Your purposes and thoughts in my mind forever. Show me anything I'm holding back, Lord. I want You to have it all.

EVENING

BEING CONSIDERATE

Understand this, my dear brothers and sisters: You must all be quick to listen, slow to speak, and slow to get angry.
JAMES 1:19 NLT

Lord, I admit it—I'm usually thinking of myself instead of someone else. Help me be more considerate of others. Help me listen when someone is speaking—*really* listen to what they're saying. Then show me what You want me to say when it's my turn to say something back.

DAY 315

MORNING

DEEP SURRENDER

But now, O LORD, You are our Father; we are the clay, and You our potter; and all we are the work of Your hand.

ISAIAH 64:8 NKJV

Lord, I need to surrender to You. You've shown me a part of my life that I've been trying to rule. Surrender means I give You permission to change me and mold me exactly the way You want. Surrender is never easy, but it's the path to true joy. Thank You for showing me this truth.

EVENING

TINY STEPS

"And if anyone gives even a cup of cold water to one of these little ones who is my disciple, truly I tell you, that person will certainly not lose their reward."

MATTHEW 10:42 NIV

Jesus, You've promised that even the smallest act done out of love for You has an eternal reward. Don't let anything stop me from doing kind things. Tiny steps now may lead to large ones later. Help me reach out to people who need Your love.

MORNING

A TRUTHFUL HEART

LORD, who may dwell in your sacred tent? Who may live on your holy mountain? The one whose walk is blameless, who does what is righteous, who speaks the truth from their heart.

PSALM 15:1–2 NIV

Lord, sometimes I lie to myself. Sometimes I try to lie to You. But You know me. You know my thoughts before I think them. Show me Your truth so that my prayers will be genuine. Show me how to live a blameless life.

EVENING

SERVE ONE ANOTHER

But through love serve one another. For all the law is fulfilled in one word, even in this: "You shall love your neighbor as yourself."

GALATIANS 5:13–14 NKJV

Father God, sometimes I forget that it's not all about me! Life is about loving You and loving others. Give me opportunities to show Your love. Help me to recognize "God moments" throughout my day and to see what other people need. Create in me a heart that loves others like I love myself.

MORNING

HIS WORK

"The Lord watches over those who are right with Him. He hears their prayers."
1 PETER 3:12 NLV

Father, I'm amazed that You never get tired of listening to me. You hear the same fears, complaints, problems, and confusions over and over. Thank You that You are always ready to listen to me. And even more than that, thank You that You keep working on me, faithfully, patiently, lovingly. You're the potter; I'm the clay in Your hands. Amen.

EVENING

USE ME, LORD

"If you try to hang on to your life, you will lose it. But if you give up your life for my sake and for the sake of the Good News, you will save it."
MARK 8:35 NLT

Jesus, You died on a cross—the kind of torture reserved for the worst criminals. But You'd done nothing wrong. You came into the world to save us! You gave Your life for us. Lord Jesus, take my life and use it for Your glory.

MORNING

ALL OF US TOGETHER

Then all of you together can thank the God and Father of our Lord Jesus Christ.
ROMANS 15:6 NLV

Lord, sometimes I struggle to get along with other people—even kids who go to the same church as I do. We don't always think the same way. But I know You want Christians to be united. Forgive me if I've done anything to pull people apart. Show me how to love people the way You do. Show me how we can worship You together.

EVENING

ALL THE GOOD THINGS

Then you and the Levites and the foreigners residing among you shall rejoice in all the good things the LORD your God has given to you and your household.
DEUTERONOMY 26:11 NIV

Father God, thank You for the blessings You've heaped on my family. Sometimes I think about what we don't have. Please remind me to be grateful. Thank You for giving us *sooo* much. Help me have a thankful heart so my whole family might be more thankful too.

MORNING

BELIEVING

"Do not be unbelieving, but believing."
JOHN 20:27 NKJV

I believe in You, Jesus. I believe in Your power and wisdom and love. I believe that Your death on the cross made a way for me to be forgiven of my sins and reconciled with God. Teach me to trust You, not asking for proof like Thomas, one of Your disciples, did—but believing You because of Your Word. Thank You for giving life to me and everyone who believes.

EVENING

A SAFE PLACE

My people will live in peaceful dwelling places,
in secure homes, in undisturbed places of rest.
ISAIAH 32:18 NIV

Lord, I know this world isn't always safe, so please protect me and my family and our home. You are always a safe place for us, no matter where we live. I'm looking forward to the time when You come back to earth and remake the whole world. Then we'll get to live with You forever. Thanks for being our security! Amen.

MORNING

ENDURANCE REQUIRED

Let us run with endurance the race that is set before us.

HEBREWS 12:1 NKJV

Lord, I'm learning that this Christian life requires endurance. Becoming like You doesn't happen all at once. It's a one-day-after-another kind of thing. So please help me be patient. Help me not give up even when I make a lot of mistakes. Remind me that You forgive me when I ask and that You're right here running the race beside me. More than anything, I want to finish well!

EVENING

GOD'S GRASP

"And this is the will of him who sent me,
that I shall lose none of all those he has
given me, but raise them up at the last day."

JOHN 6:39 NIV

Father God, I might lose things—like my homework or my phone—but You never do. For sure, You'll never lose me. I'm Yours forever. Any heart You hold, You grasp firmly in Your hand. Thank You, Lord, for holding me tight and loving me so much.

MORNING

THE GRAND TIMELINE

He has made everything beautiful in its time. He has put thoughts of the forever in man's mind, yet man cannot understand the work God has done from the beginning to the end.
ECCLESIASTES 3:11 NLV

Creator God, the grand story of history is really *Your* story. You thought of the end from the very beginning, and I know I can trust You with my whole life. Thank You for Your perfect timing and the promise of forever with You.

EVENING

A HEART AT PEACE

A heart at peace gives life to the body, but envy rots the bones.
PROVERBS 14:30 NIV

Lord, when my heart is restless, always wanting more and more, I don't feel great physically. But when I'm content, You seem to restore my whole body. I can breathe easier, I can relax, and I can smile again because I know everything's going to be all right. I'm all right because You're in control. Help me have a heart that's at peace.

MORNING

JOY IN THE MORNING

"For the joy of the LORD is your strength."
NEHEMIAH 8:10 NIV

Father God, some mornings I wake up ready to go! I feel energized. Other mornings, I wonder how I'll get to the end of the day. Remind me that I have a power source that is always available to me. I may not always feel joyful, but the joy of the Lord is my strength. Lord, as I read the Bible this morning, please recharge me. In Jesus' name I pray. Amen.

EVENING

TWO ARE BETTER THAN ONE

Two are better than one; because they have a good reward for their labour. For if they fall, the one will lift up his fellow.
ECCLESIASTES 4:9–10 KJV

Heavenly Father, You tell us in Your Word that it's not good to be alone. We all need somebody to pick us up when we're down. So I'm asking You to bring good friends into my life. Help me make friendship one of the most important parts of my life.

MORNING

TRUE JOY

"These things I have spoken to you, that My joy may remain in you, and that your joy may be full."
JOHN 15:11 NKJV

Jesus, this world sends me a lot of messages through the media and through people who don't know You. I've tried some of the things that are supposed to bring joy, but they always leave me empty. Thank You for the truth. Help me stick close to You so I'll be full of joy. Amen.

EVENING

SHIELD OF FAITH

In addition to all of these, hold up the shield of faith to stop the fiery arrows of the devil.
EPHESIANS 6:16 NLT

Father God, guard my heart and mind with the shield of faith. I'll call out to You when Satan tempts me. I'll fight against his schemes. My weapon is the Bible, verses I've memorized and hold tight. My defense is my faith in Jesus, my Savior. Please increase my faith, Lord, and protect me from the evil one.

MORNING

HELP WITH PRIORITIES

"For where your treasure is,
there your heart will be also."
MATTHEW 6:21 NIV

Dear God, I need help with my priorities. It's so easy for them to get out of whack. Show me the things I've let creep to the top that don't belong there. Point out to me where I need to be more committed. Help me remember that people are worth more than things or achievements, and let my priorities reflect that fact.

EVENING

FRIENDS HELP EACH OTHER

If either of them falls down, one can help the other up.
But pity anyone who falls and has no one to help them up.
ECCLESIASTES 4:10 NIV

Lord, I want to be a giver, to help my friends when they need it. Help me learn to receive too—so that I'm not too proud to accept help from a friend when *I* need it. Give and take, Lord. . . we really do need each other.

DAY 325

MORNING

DON'T WORRY!

Don't worry about anything;
instead, pray about everything.
PHILIPPIANS 4:6 NLT

Dear Lord, the Bible tells me it's wrong to worry. Some people say they're just born worriers. Maybe there's some truth to that—some people really do worry a lot more than others. Still, You know worry isn't good for us and doesn't get anything done. So, today, help me not to worry. Help me turn to You instead and pray about everything.

EVENING

FIGHTING DISCOURAGEMENT

"Then you will have success if you are careful to observe
the decrees and laws that the LORD gave Moses for Israel.
Be strong and courageous. Do not be afraid or discouraged."
1 CHRONICLES 22:13 NIV

Discouragement makes me feel so empty inside, Lord, but You remind me that You'll give me strength. I have no reason to dread. When I feel weak and cry out to You for help, Your power will fill me. You'll win the fight against fear as I put my trust in You.

MORNING

EXTRAS

And my God will meet all your needs according to the riches of his glory in Christ Jesus.

PHILIPPIANS 4:19 NIV

Dear God, I'm so thankful for the ways You've provided for me. So many times Your blessings even go above and beyond my needs. Help me know how to handle these gifts. I want to make sure I'm not controlled by the stuff I have. Instead, I want to glorify You. Please help me use Your extras in a way that honors You.

EVENING

THE PATIENCE CHALLENGE

Love is patient, love is kind.

1 CORINTHIANS 13:4 NIV

My love isn't always patient, Lord. Sometimes people just seem extra difficult to love. But You're always patient and kind. Even when I haven't deserved it, You've given me second chances. I want to reflect that sort of love, the sort You pour out on me. I might not be very good at showing it right now, but I'll keep trying! With Your help, I'll grow in love and patience.

DAY 327

MORNING

A RIGHT OUTLOOK

He who loves money will never have enough money to make him happy. It is the same for the one who loves to get many things. This also is for nothing.
ECCLESIASTES 5:10 NLV

Father God, I wonder how often money is the cause of problems between people. Some people are careless or dishonest. Other people just want too much. Whatever the case, jealousy, hatred, greed, and selfishness all result from a wrong view of money. Lord, please help me have Your perspective on money.

EVENING

ALWAYS

Rejoice always, pray without ceasing, in everything give thanks; for this is the will of God in Christ Jesus for you.
1 THESSALONIANS 5:16–18 NKJV

Lord, some days I want to shout about what You're doing. Other days I feel bored and can't think of anything to rejoice about, much less give thanks for! Help me be joyful and thankful every day because that's how You want me to live—and that's how I want to live too.

MORNING

THE LITTLE ONES

"In the same way your Father in heaven is not willing that any of these little ones should perish."
MATTHEW 18:14 NIV

Lord, I'm so glad we don't have to be famous or extra-important for You to care about us. You told a parable about a shepherd leaving his flock to look for one lost sheep. That's how You see us—important enough to go after, no matter who we are. Thank You for loving *me* so much!

EVENING

INCORRUPTIBLE BEAUTY

Let it be the hidden person of the heart, with the incorruptible beauty of a gentle and quiet spirit, which is very precious in the sight of God.
1 PETER 3:4 NKJV

God, in Your eyes a gentle and quiet spirit is worth more than gold. It's forever. Please give me a spirit like that. Help me choose what I say carefully. Teach me to walk humbly with You and to serve people in Your name. Amen.

DAY 329

MORNING

IN CHRIST ALONE

"Salvation is found in no one else,
for there is no other name under heaven given
to mankind by which we must be saved."
ACTS 4:12 NIV

Lord Jesus, salvation required a huge sacrifice on Your part, but now it's freely available to us. Yet a lot of people still try to save themselves. Other people don't think they need saving at all. Lord, I'm so thankful to depend on You and not myself or anyone else to save me.

EVENING

GOD'S AMAZING GIFT

For the grace of God has appeared
that offers salvation to all people.
TITUS 2:11 NIV

Heavenly Father, thank You for the gift of salvation, for sending Your only Son to be a sacrifice for all people. I'm in awe of Your mercy. To think that I'm a daughter of God is mind-blowing. Thank You, Holy Spirit, for drawing me to this great gift—the greatest gift ever. I don't want to imagine my life without it. Amen!

MORNING

ACCORDING TO HIS PLAN

[God] has saved us and called us with a holy calling, not according to our works, but according to His own purpose and grace which was given to us in Christ Jesus before time began.

2 TIMOTHY 1:9 NKJV

Father God, before You spoke the world into existence, You had me in mind. You had a plan. You gave Your Son to pay for my sins! I can't totally understand how deep Your love is, but I'm so thankful for it.

EVENING

MIGHTY THINGS

"Call to Me, and I will answer you, and show you great and mighty things, which you do not know."

JEREMIAH 33:3 NKJV

Forgive me, Lord, for neglecting prayer. I get busy, and I end up shortchanging You. Some days I don't pray at all, Lord. Make me faithful to spend time with You. Thank You for wanting to share great and mighty things with me from Your Word. I'm calling on You now, waiting for You to impart Your wisdom to my heart.

DAY 331

MORNING

UNLIMITED RESOURCES

The next day we landed at Sidon; and Julius, in kindness to Paul, allowed him to go to his friends so they might provide for his needs.

ACTS 27:3 NIV

Lord, Your resources are unlimited. You love giving Your kids everything they need and much more. Today, Lord, I'm asking You to meet the needs of my church. Show me ways that I can help, just like Paul's friends helped him. I know You won't let us down.

EVENING

STEWARDSHIP

The LORD is my strength and my shield; my heart trusts in him, and he helps me. My heart leaps for joy, and with my song I praise him.

PSALM 28:7 NIV

Lord, You've given me so many things—things I can hold in my hands but also talents and time. Help me take care of and use everything You've entrusted to me. Help me be a good steward. I trust You always, because You are my strength, my shield, my joy.

MORNING

A HEART TO SERVE

The LORD is gracious and compassionate,
slow to anger and rich in love.
PSALM 145:8 NIV

Lord, I pray for a spirit like Yours—a spirit of compassion. Motivate me to care about what other people are going through and what they need. Help me genuinely love them. Make me a blessing to them. Show me exactly where I can serve You by serving people in Your name. May they see Your grace and compassion through me.

EVENING

A FATHER'S COMPASSION

As a father has compassion on his children, so the
LORD has compassion on those who fear him.
PSALM 103:13 NIV

Dear Lord, help me remember that You're my Father. A heavenly Father—one who has unlimited power and infinitely more love than any earthly father. Please fill my heart with the truth that You love me perfectly and have only the best in mind for me. You want to embrace me, bless me, and give me all of heaven. You're amazing!

DAY 333

MORNING

REIGNING PEACE

"I have told you all this so that you may have peace in me. Here on earth you will have many trials and sorrows. But take heart, because I have overcome the world."

JOHN 16:33 NLT

Dear God, I pray for peace around the world. Some say it's impossible—but with You all things are possible. And even if peace doesn't reign in the world, with You in my heart, peace reigns inside me. All because You've overcome the world!

EVENING

NEVER GIVE UP

Therefore, my dear friends, as you have always obeyed—not only in my presence, but now much more in my absence—continue to work out your salvation with fear and trembling, for it is God who works in you to will and to act in order to fulfill his good purpose.

PHILIPPIANS 2:12–13 NIV

Lord, I don't want to be a quitter, but I keep messing up. Please don't let me give up. Help me remember that You're not finished working.

MORNING

REAL SUCCESS

Commit to the LORD whatever you do,
and he will establish your plans.
PROVERBS 16:3 NIV

Lord, please bless what I do today. I commit my plans to You and surrender my will for Yours. Help me see what Your plans are for my life, and show me what real success looks like for me. In everything I dream of doing, in everything I hope to become someday, may *our* plans succeed. With You behind them, they will!

EVENING

SETTING GOALS

For wisdom is better than rubies; and all the things
that may be desired are not to be compared to it.
PROVERBS 8:11 KJV

Sometimes I get discouraged, Lord Jesus. I feel like I've accomplished all the goals I've set for myself and there's nothing for me to aim toward right now. Please give me a new outlook. Give me wisdom as I set new goals, and help me give You the glory when I reach them. Amen.

DAY 335

MORNING

WHO'S THE BOSS?

I trust in God, so why should I be afraid? What can mere mortals do to me? I will fulfill my vows to you, O God, and will offer a sacrifice of thanks for your help.

PSALM 56:11–12 NLT

Lord, I pray for a right mindset with my teacher. Help me listen and work with honesty. At the same time, help me remember that You're my highest authority. My ultimate trust is in You, and You're above everybody.

EVENING

POWERFUL AND EFFECTIVE

The prayer of a righteous person is powerful and effective.

JAMES 5:16 NIV

A good prayer is worth a lot in Your eyes, Father. I know how much prayers have helped me—and not just the ones I've prayed. Thank You for people who have prayed for me when I needed it. I want to pray powerfully and effectively too, to pass on the blessing. So many people need it. Help me be right with You so I can.

MORNING

CONTINUALLY CONTENT

I am not saying this because I am in need, for I have learned to be content whatever the circumstances.

PHILIPPIANS 4:11 NIV

Lord, I dream a lot about the future, but I can only live right now. Please help me be content with today, no matter what my circumstances are. Whatever my life looks like, I can turn to You for peace. Calm me and comfort me so that wherever I go today and tomorrow, I will be content. Amen.

EVENING

MEEKNESS

Live and work without pride. Be gentle and kind. Do not be hard on others. Let love keep you from doing that.

EPHESIANS 4:2 NLV

Heavenly Father, I want to develop the characteristic of meekness, a kind of quiet strength. It takes guts to be silent when you want to speak. It takes strength to be kind when other people aren't. It takes You helping me to be like that. So please help me learn how to be meek but strong.

DAY 337

MORNING

WHOSE APPROVAL?

Am I now trying to win the approval of human beings, or of God? Or am I trying to please people? If I were still trying to please people, I would not be a servant of Christ.

GALATIANS 1:10 NIV

Lord, teach me to center my thoughts and actions on You and to keep my focus. You've never asked me to please everyone. You're the one I look to for approval. You're the one I want to please in everything I do.

EVENING

WHAT LASTS

Prophecy and speaking in unknown languages and special knowledge will become useless. But love will last forever!

1 CORINTHIANS 13:8 NLT

Father God, I can spend my time on a lot of things, on really good things, but not many of them will be around forever. Help me love people more—just like You love people—because love is the only lasting thing on earth. It lasts all the way to heaven! Even when I'm gone, love will stick around.

MORNING

REST WITHOUT STRESS

Do not be anxious about anything, but in every situation, by prayer and petition, with thanksgiving, present your requests to God.

PHILIPPIANS 4:6 NIV

Lord, I'm feeling a lot of pressure at school right now—too many tests and too much homework. Help me do what needs to be done each day so I can stop worrying. I give You my stress. Cover me with Your peace, and guard my heart and mind. I rest in Your love.

EVENING

NEVER ALONE

"Be strong and of good courage, do not fear nor be afraid of them; for the LORD your God, He is the One who goes with you. He will not leave you nor forsake you."

DEUTERONOMY 31:6 NKJV

It would be easy to give in to fear, Lord, but You remind me that I'm not walking through life alone. Thank You for standing by me no matter what. When I put all my fears in Your hands, I know I'm safe.

DAY 339

MORNING

JOYFUL SERVANT

"Well done, my good and faithful servant. You have been faithful in handling this small amount, so now I will give you many more responsibilities. Let's celebrate together!"

MATTHEW 25:23 NLT

Father God, I want to be a good and faithful servant, but I feel like the world is bringing me down. Help me be faithful with what You've given me. Teach me what that looks like. I want to feel—and share—the joy that comes from working for You.

EVENING

CONSULTING CHRIST

Trust in the LORD with all your heart,
and lean not on your own understanding.

PROVERBS 3:5 NKJV

Lord, sometimes when I'm planning out my day, I forget to check in with You. Then I wonder why things don't work out the way I think they should. Please forgive my arrogant attitude. I know I'll be truly happy only when I allow You to guide me through the day. Show me how to align my goals with Your will.

MORNING

THE WORK OF MY HANDS

The LORD your God will bless you in all your harvest and in all the work of your hands, and your joy will be complete.
DEUTERONOMY 16:15 NIV

Lord, whatever I do today—like finishing my science project or cleaning my room or helping Mom with dinner—please bless the work of my hands. Help me be cheerful even when the work is a drag. I dedicate my work and my day to You, Lord. Amen.

EVENING

PRAYER POWER

The Lord is far from the sinful, but He hears the prayer of those who are right with Him.
PROVERBS 15:29 NLV

Father God, talking to You infuses my life with power. When I turn to You, I tap into Your strength. You might not answer me exactly the way I expected, but You've always answered me the way I needed You to. Please draw me close to You. Thank You for hearing every one of my prayers.

DAY 341

MORNING

THE RIGHT ATTITUDE

Do everything without complaining and arguing.
PHILIPPIANS 2:14 NLT

I'm getting tired of school, Lord. It seems like the same thing every day. . .all week long. I can't seem to get past this negativity I'm feeling. Lord, give me the right mindset even before I go to class. And then remind me that I'm working for You. Please give me the mind and attitude of Jesus today, and help me keep it all day long. Amen.

EVENING

SENSORY JOYS

For in him we live, and move, and have our being.
ACTS 17:28 KJV

Dear God, thank You for the five senses—sight, hearing, touch, smell, and taste. You could have designed a virtual world, but instead You created one that can be experienced. Today I want to celebrate the fact that I'm alive—that I can see and hear and feel and smell and taste. I want to enjoy these gifts that come straight from You.

MORNING

RESPONDING WELL TO CRITICISM

A fool is quick-tempered, but a wise person stays calm when insulted.
PROVERBS 12:16 NLT

Lord, I don't like being criticized. If the criticism is from someone who cares about me, help me hear what they're saying. But if the criticism is just hate—someone saying bad things about me—help me stay calm. Please remind me what's really true when others are spreading lies. Make me patient so I will not lash out but respond like You would.

EVENING

GOSSIP

Put out of your life all these things: bad feelings about other people, anger, temper, loud talk, bad talk which hurts other people, and bad feelings which hurt other people.
EPHESIANS 4:31 NLV

Lord, I got caught in gossip today. I tried to stop listening but didn't try hard enough. Please forgive me. Give me the courage to make the right decision next time. Help me refuse to listen to negative stories about someone who isn't there to defend herself. Amen.

DAY 343

MORNING

A NEW MINDSET

Let God transform you into a new person by changing the way you think. Then you will learn to know God's will for you, which is good and pleasing and perfect.

ROMANS 12:2 NLT

I have the wrong mindset today, Lord. Instead of looking to You, I'm focused on the world. That's not where You want my mind to be. Please change my thoughts and my desires. I want to live a life that is good and pleasing to You.

EVENING

FORGIVENESS AND HEALING

Let all that I am praise the LORD; may I never forget the good things he does for me. He forgives all my sins and heals all my diseases.

PSALM 103:2–3 NLT

Father God, You've forgiven my sins and healed my soul. You do amazing things for me. Nothing is impossible with You in my life. Thank You for taking care of me. With all that I am, with my entire being, I praise You forever and ever!

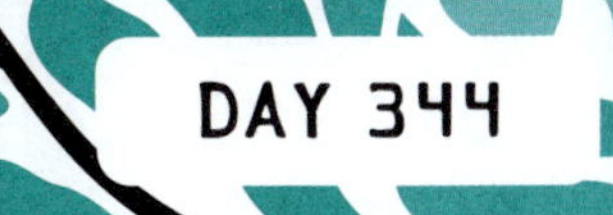

MORNING

SPIRIT-FILLED

"I have filled him with the Spirit of God, giving him great wisdom, ability, and expertise in all kinds of crafts."

EXODUS 31:3 NLT

Father God, You've filled me with Your Holy Spirit and equipped me for life. Show me how I can use my knowledge and abilities to do what You've planned out for me. What do You want me to do with my hands, my gifts, my life? They all come from You, Lord, the one I want to serve.

EVENING

GOD'S INSTRUCTIONS

And God wanted good to come to them, saying, "Give birth to many. Grow in number. Fill the earth and rule over it. Rule over the fish of the sea, over the birds of the sky, and over every living thing that moves on the earth."

GENESIS 1:28 NLV

Lord God, part of Your instructions to people was to watch over the earth. I want to learn about Your creation so I can treasure the amazing things You've made. Amen.

DAY 345

MORNING

MAKING ALLOWANCES

Make allowance for each other's faults, and forgive anyone who offends you. Remember, the Lord forgave you, so you must forgive others.

COLOSSIANS 3:13 NLT

Nobody's perfect, Lord. I know that, but sometimes I struggle to just get over it when people hurt my feelings. When I'm stuck in unforgiveness, remind me that I'm not perfect either. I've hurt people too, sometimes without even knowing it. I've hurt *You*. But, Father God, You always forgive. Help me forgive like You do.

EVENING

HAVE FAITH

"You can pray for anything, and if you have faith, you will receive it."

MATTHEW 21:22 NLT

Lord, You promise that if I have faith, I'll receive. But sometimes my faith seems so small, all I can do is ask for Your help to believe. Help me trust You more. Help me know You more so that whatever I ask for is what You want too. Then it will be easy to have faith so that when I ask, I'll receive.

MORNING

A TESTIMONY

He has put a new song in my mouth—praise to our God; many will see it and fear, and will trust in the LORD.

PSALM 40:3 NKJV

My life is a song of praise to You, Lord! When people hear me talk about how good and awesome You are, I hope they'll get to know You more. I want people to notice how You fill my life with joy and peace so I can point them to You. Amen.

EVENING

A PRAYER FOR PRISONERS

"I was in prison and you came to visit me."

MATTHEW 25:36 NIV

Lord, I'm praying for the men and women in prison all over our country. Please help them know You like I know You. You want us to have hope and peace in every situation. You want to forgive and love us. Lord, I'm also praying for believers who are imprisoned around the world because they believe in You. Show me how I can encourage them.

MORNING

MORNING MEDITATION

Hear my cry for help, my King and my God, for to you I pray. In the morning, LORD, you hear my voice; in the morning I lay my requests before you and wait expectantly.

PSALM 5:2–3 NIV

Father God, You love me and lead me. How great is that! This morning I'm sending my prayers to You, knowing You'll hear my words and understand what I'm saying (and even what I'm *not* saying). I'm giving You my requests and waiting eagerly for Your answers.

EVENING

MUSIC

Whatever you do, do everything to honor God.

1 CORINTHIANS 10:31 NLV

Lord, music is part of every culture everywhere. It's a huge part of my life and my friends' lives. But I want my music choices to honor You. Music affects my mood, my attitude, even my spirit, so I want to listen to music that's good for me—music that goes along with what You're doing in me.

MORNING

THE GOOD SHEPHERD

The LORD is my shepherd.
PSALM 23:1 NIV

My shepherd, lead me next to still waters. Guide me to green pastures. With You by my side, I won't fear anything. You're my comfort and my provider. I'm happy when You're near—and You're *always* near. Your goodness and mercy are with me right now and forever. Lord, thank You for leading me here and watching over me—for being the shepherd of my life.

EVENING

HOMEWORK HELP

Seek his will in all you do, and he will show you which path to take.
PROVERBS 3:6 NLT

Father God, I feel like I've been staring at my homework for hours. I'm supposed to come up with a project idea before tomorrow, but no ideas are coming to mind. . .all I have is a blank piece of paper! I know You want me to do a good job. I know You want to help me with everything. Please show me what to do.

MORNING

MY EVERYTHING

"'Love the Lord your God with all your heart and with all your soul and with all your mind.' This is the first and greatest commandment."

MATTHEW 22:37–38 NIV

Father God, You are the most important thing in my life! You made me. You adore me. You guide me and provide for me. Forgive me when I let things interrupt our relationship, Lord. Help me spend more time with You, especially in the mornings. I love You so much! I don't ever want to let You down.

EVENING

SPECIAL INSTRUCTIONS

Your word is a lamp to my feet and a light to my path.

PSALM 119:105 NKJV

Thank You for the Bible, Lord. I would never know how to be like You or how to live in a way that pleases You without it. Thank You for ensuring Your words were passed from generation to generation so I can read them today and find a way through my problems. Help me memorize the verses You highlight for me. Help me walk them out.

MORNING

GOD'S GLORY, NOT MINE

*Do everything that way,
heartily and freely to God's glory.*
1 CORINTHIANS 10:31 MSG

I want everything I do today to be for You, Lord. I don't want my actions to be about getting attention or just having fun. I'm here on earth for You. Help me not to be so busy or wrapped up in myself that I don't have time for You and the things You're asking me to do. Give me energy for every task, Lord, and remind me to give You the glory when I'm done.

EVENING

BURDENS LIFTED

*"Come to me, all you who are weary
and burdened, and I will give you rest."*
MATTHEW 11:28 NIV

Lord, I don't want to be burdened—like a mule carrying a huge pack up a mountain. That's why I'm so thankful You offer to take my burdens. You promise to lift the weight and give me rest. Take all my sins and doubts, Lord, and exchange them for Your peace. Fill my heart with trust in my burden bearer—You!

DAY 351

MORNING

WITH HIM EACH MOMENT

"Seek the Kingdom of God above all else, and live righteously, and he will give you everything you need."
MATTHEW 6:33 NLT

Calm my heart, Lord. Help me breathe slower. I want to relax here, just sitting with You like two friends hanging out. You are my best friend, Jesus! You're with me every minute of my day; and through Your grace, each part of my life—the good and the bad—is woven into a beautiful tapestry pointing to Your goodness.

EVENING

A BLESSING OF PEACE

"The LORD bless you and keep you; the LORD make his face shine on you and be gracious to you; the LORD turn his face toward you and give you peace."
NUMBERS 6:24–26 NIV

Lord, long ago You told Moses to bless the Israelites with these words. Today I ask that You'd bless me with peace as I pray this prayer. Let Your love and mercy shine on me so I can be a light that shines for others.

MORNING

RELENTLESS PRAYING

[Daniel] prayed three times a day, just as he had always done, giving thanks to his God.

DANIEL 6:10 NLT

"Just as he had always done"—I needed those words today, Father. Help me be like Daniel. When all seemed bleak and hopeless in his world, he didn't panic but kept worshipping You. He continued to pray to You three times a day, just as he'd always done. Lord, keep me close to You just as You always have.

EVENING

THINGS NOT SEEN

Now faith is confidence in what we hope for and assurance about what we do not see.

HEBREWS 11:1 NIV

Lord Jesus, sometimes I wish I could reach out and touch You. As I think about Your words in the Bible, I realize it's easy to believe in things I can see. Please give me faith to believe in things I *can't* see. Give me faith that all Your promises are true and that one day You'll return to earth to take me home. Amen.

MORNING

ONE-TOUCH HEALING

For she thought, "If I can just touch his robe, I will be healed."
MATTHEW 9:21 NLT

Lord Jesus, I'm reaching out my hand to You, knowing if I can just touch the edge of Your robe, You'll make me whole. I imagine You in front of me. I see the kindness in Your eyes. I know that You love me and that nothing is impossible for You. Fill me with Your love. Heal my heart with just a touch.

EVENING

THE GOAL IS LOVE

The goal of this command is love, which comes from a pure heart and a good conscience and a sincere faith.
1 TIMOTHY 1:5 NIV

Father God, love is Your greatest commandment, and I want it to be my greatest aim. Fill me with Your kind of unconditional love, and empower me to really care about other people. I want the love I share to come from a pure heart and not from any selfish motives. Amen.

MORNING

KEEP THOSE PRIORITIES STRAIGHT

"God is with you in all that you do."
GENESIS 21:22 NKJV

Lord, as I go through my day, help me keep my priorities straight—to keep the important things important. How I treat other people matters so much more than what I do. Help me be kind and considerate. When people see me, I want them to recognize You, because that's what the world needs more of than anything else—Your love, Your presence, Your light.

EVENING

THE FAITHFUL ONE

But the Lord is faithful. He will give you strength and keep you safe from the devil.
2 THESSALONIANS 3:3 NLV

Lord God, I focus a lot on my faith in You. And then You show me that it's not all about me. You're so faithful to me and show me how to be faithful. You never give up on me. You never leave. You never turn away. You always show up. Thank You for Your faithfulness in my life. Amen.

MORNING

BEARING FRUIT

That person is like a tree planted by streams of water, which yields its fruit in season and whose leaf does not wither—whatever they do prospers.

PSALM 1:3 NIV

God, I come to You this morning thinking about Your Word. The Bible is my daily bread, just as You are my living water, the quencher of my thirst. You provide everything for me. All day today, whatever I'm doing, please help me do it well and for Your great glory! Amen.

EVENING

UNTROUBLED

The fear of the LORD leads to life; then one rests content, untouched by trouble.

PROVERBS 19:23 NIV

Lord, You're powerful beyond anything my mind can imagine. I don't need to be afraid of You, though. You've made me Your child, and that makes all the difference. Because I respect You and live for You, I can rest. I can relax. I can be content, because I'm trusting in You to take care of all my needs—every single one.

MORNING

MY FIRST DESIRE

One thing I have asked from the Lord, that I will look for: that I may live in the house of the Lord all the days of my life, to look upon the beauty of the Lord, and to worship in His holy house.

PSALM 27:4 NLV

Lord, help me keep the main thing front and center—and that's to seek You and Your ways. No matter how busy I get, may I always ask to be with You.

EVENING

BEING GODLY ON PURPOSE

Don't copy the behavior and customs of this world, but let God transform you into a new person by changing the way you think. Then you will learn to know God's will for you.

ROMANS 12:2 NLT

Lord, godly character doesn't just happen, does it? I have to decide to let You change me. Only then will I not cave to peer pressure. Only then will I live the way You want me to. That's my prayer tonight, Lord. Please transform me!

DAY 357

MORNING

A NEW DAY

Anxiety weighs down the heart,
but a kind word cheers it up.
PROVERBS 12:25 NIV

Here I am, Lord, getting ready for another day. Help me stay calm and not get caught up in drama—all that stress isn't worth it. Help me focus on You. Help me keep Your words of peace and love up front in my mind today so my heart will be happy. And help me cheer up my friends so their hearts can be happy too.

EVENING

RESTING ON THE SABBATH

"Remember to observe the Sabbath day by keeping it holy. You have six days each week for your ordinary work, but the seventh day is a Sabbath day of rest dedicated to the LORD your God. On that day no one in your household may do any work."
EXODUS 20:8–10 NLT

Father God, resting one day a week seems kind of old-fashioned, but You want me to pattern my life after You. You took a break—and so will I!

MORNING

I WILL FOLLOW YOU

Then he said to them all: "Whoever wants to be my disciple must deny themselves and take up their cross daily and follow me. For whoever wants to save their life will lose it, but whoever loses their life for me will save it."

LUKE 9:23–24 NIV

Lord, please show me what "taking up my cross" and "losing my life" look like. Teach me about surrender so that I can be prepared when You lift me up to do great things.

EVENING

SAVED BY GRACE

For it is by grace you have been saved, through faith—and this is not from yourselves, it is the gift of God—not by works, so that no one can boast.

EPHESIANS 2:8–9 NIV

Father God, when You look at me, You see Jesus in me. You see not sin but righteousness. I couldn't have earned that no matter how hard I worked. You saved me freely because of Your grace and love. Have I thanked You yet today?

MORNING

LET'S GROW

Like newborn babies, crave pure spiritual milk, so that by it you may grow up in your salvation.
1 PETER 2:2 NIV

Lord, I want to grow up spiritually. I want to learn more and more about You, craving Your words and Your presence like a newborn baby cries for milk. I want to move from head knowledge to heart experience with You. Step by step and day by day, teach me Your ways and how to follow You.

EVENING

THE CENTER OF GOD'S WILL

Commit to the LORD whatever you do, and he will establish your plans.
PROVERBS 16:3 NIV

Lord, I know that peace and joy and countless other blessings are in the center of Your will—they come when I follow Your ways. The trouble I have sometimes is figuring out what Your will for me actually is. Please help me listen when You speak, and give me a heart willing to be used by You. Amen.

MORNING

GOD'S PRESENCE

"The virgin will conceive and give birth to a son, and they will call him Immanuel" (which means "God with us").

MATTHEW 1:23 NIV

Heavenly Father, thank You for sending Jesus—Immanuel, God with us. Jesus lived on this earth—in towns with all kinds of people—so He could point to the truth and make a relationship with You possible. Thank You for Jesus—and for Your Spirit who lives in me today. You are "God with me"!

EVENING

RESTING IN THE LORD

The LORD replied, "My Presence will go with you, and I will give you rest."

EXODUS 33:14 NIV

Lord, Moses needed reassurance that You would be with him when he led the Israelites. Like Moses, I'm nothing on my own. But challenging circumstances don't need to upset me much, because Your presence goes with me wherever I go. Your Spirit calms me and gives me rest even when my world is anything but peaceful. Help me rest in You always.

MORNING

RESTORED RELATIONSHIP

"We have believed in Christ Jesus, so that we might be made right with God because of our faith in Christ, not because we have obeyed the law. For no one will ever be made right with God by obeying the law."

GALATIANS 2:16 NLT

Lord, You know how painful a rift between friends can be. So I'm beyond thankful that I'm made right with You by faith. I want to live in a growing relationship with You—always.

EVENING

GRANTING FORGIVENESS

"And when you stand praying, if you hold anything against anyone, forgive them, so that your Father in heaven may forgive you your sins."

MARK 11:25 NIV

Heavenly Father, I need to forgive someone who wronged me. I know it's the right thing to do, but it's so difficult. I can't do it in my own strength. Please put Your love in my heart so I can have a forgiving attitude and a heart of mercy. I'm leaning on Your power. Amen.

MORNING

THE GIFT OF THE HOLY SPIRIT

*"You have made known to me the paths of life;
you will fill me with joy in your presence."*
ACTS 2:28 NIV

Lord, I've asked You to forgive my sins, and You have! Thank You that Your Holy Spirit now lives inside me. What a gift! Empower me to live a Spirit-filled life. Let my thoughts and actions overflow with love and light so other people will see You in me.

EVENING

CHRIST'S LONELINESS

*"Don't be afraid, for I am with you.
Don't be discouraged, for I am your God."*
ISAIAH 41:10 NLT

Lord Jesus, You must have felt alone when You were praying in the garden and the disciples fell asleep. And when the Father turned His back on You when You hung on the cross? I can't imagine how horrible that feeling of abandonment must have been! Better than anyone else, Jesus, You understand when I'm lonely; and I thank You for being there for me.

DAY 363

MORNING

THE POWER OF THE CROSS

Preaching about the cross sounds foolish to those who are dying in sin. But it is the power of God to those of us who are being saved from the punishment of sin.

1 CORINTHIANS 1:18 NLV

Lord, Your power is amazing. No one else is like You. No one else can do miracles like bringing the dead back to life and changing lives like mine. Please help more and more people to understand and experience the power of the cross.

EVENING

POWER BOOST

He gives strength to the weary and increases the power of the weak. . . . Those who hope in the LORD will renew their strength. They will soar on wings like eagles; they will run and not grow weary, they will walk and not be faint.

ISAIAH 40:29, 31 NIV

Dear Father God, I feel like a battery that has no more power. I'm relying on Your promise to give me strength. I know You will! Thanks for the power boost, Lord!

MORNING

PRAYER FOR SALVATION

If you declare with your mouth, "Jesus is Lord," and believe in your heart that God raised him from the dead, you will be saved.
ROMANS 10:9 NIV

Lord, I believe Jesus is the Son of God and that He died on a cross and was raised from the dead. He conquered death so I can live life to the fullest—here on earth and forever in heaven. Thank You for forgiving me and for being my Savior and Lord.

EVENING

TEARS

Put my tears into Your bottle; are they not in Your book?
PSALM 56:8 NKJV

I hate to cry, Lord. Sometimes I cry for no reason at all, like today. But since You read what's in my heart and know everything about me, I know You understand completely. You even cried when You lived here on earth. Thank You for valuing my tears, Lord—for caring enough about me to see them and catch them as they fall.

DAY 365

MORNING

STRONG ARMS

"The God Who lives forever is your safe place. His arms are always under you. He drove away from in front of you those who hate you, and said, 'Destroy!'"
DEUTERONOMY 33:27 NLV

Your strong arms hold me safely, Father God, even in the middle of troubles. Help me believe You're always there for me. Drive away the enemies that threaten me—whether I see them or not. I want to live and trust in You. You are my safe place!

EVENING

THANK YOU FOR SAVING ME!

Thank God for this gift too wonderful for words!
2 CORINTHIANS 9:15 NLT

Lord, thank You for salvation. Thank You for giving me eternal life and the power to live for You. I can't totally understand all You suffered, yet You did it all for me—for every person on this planet. You made a way for us. You were victorious over death so we could live. Thank You—again and again and again.

SCRIPTURE INDEX

OLD TESTAMENT

Proverbs

Ecclesiastes

Isaiah

NEW TESTAMENT

John

Acts

Romans

1 Corinthians

2 Corinthians

Galatians

Ephesians

Philippians

Colossians

1 Thessalonians

2 Thessalonians

1 Timothy

2 Timothy

Revelation